Copyright © 2024 Katty T

ISBN: 9798328153102

DEDICATED TO MY MUSE
THE SKY

# Author's Note

I've always had a wild imagination, lingering
on symbols, shapes and meanings.

My friends couldn't see what I saw.
The very reason I am inviting them right now,
to the world of my imagination, so they can
see the other part of me.

You're invited too!

Train your imagination to the realm of the
impossible before you make it possible.

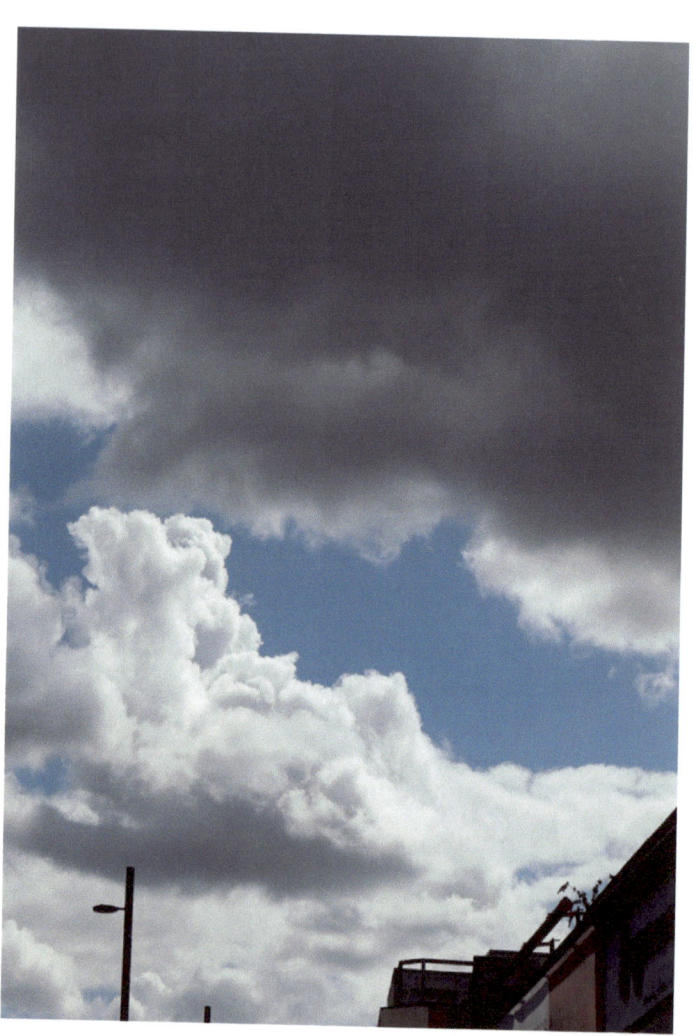

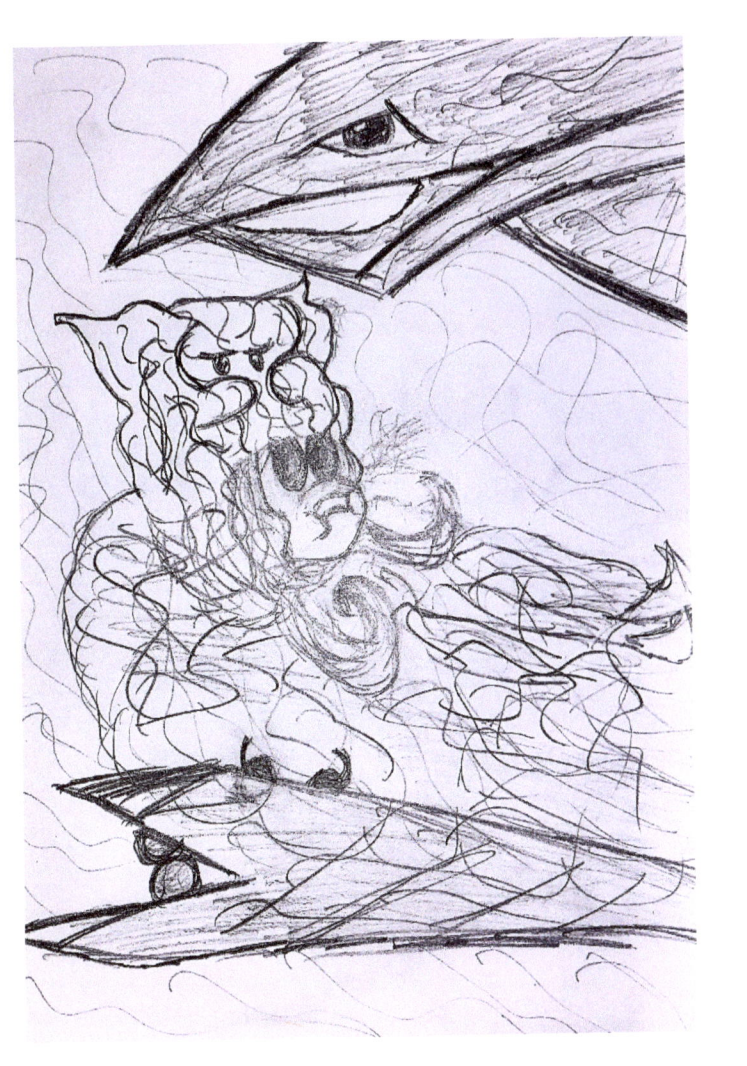

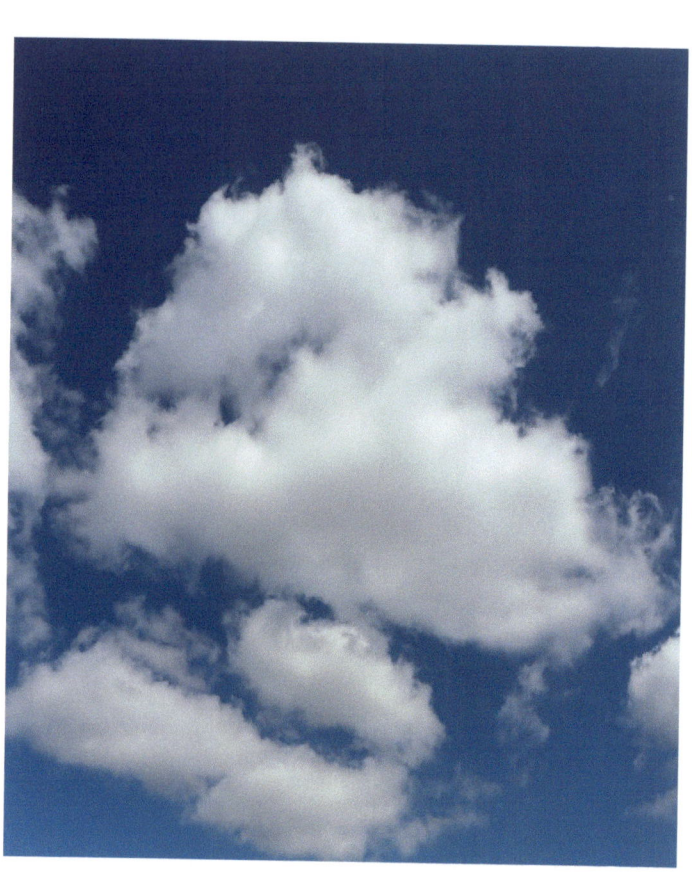

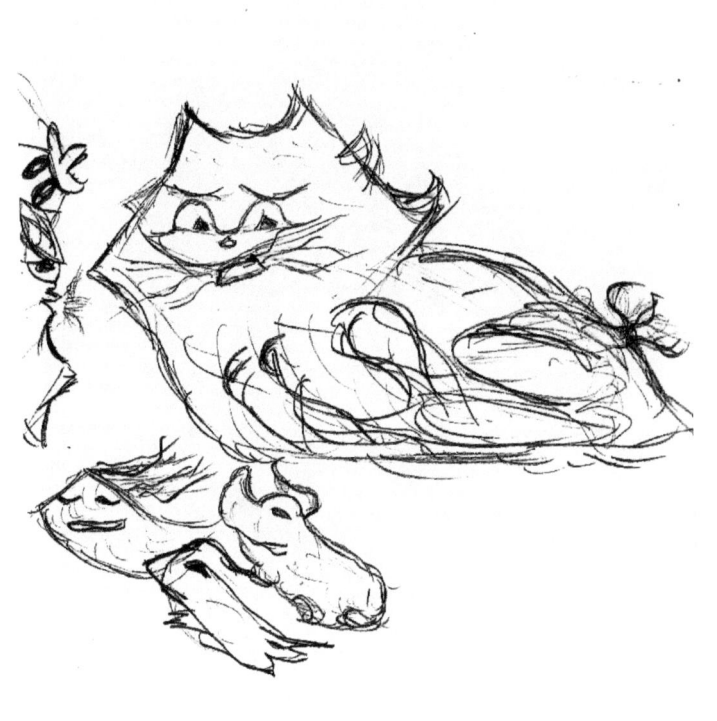

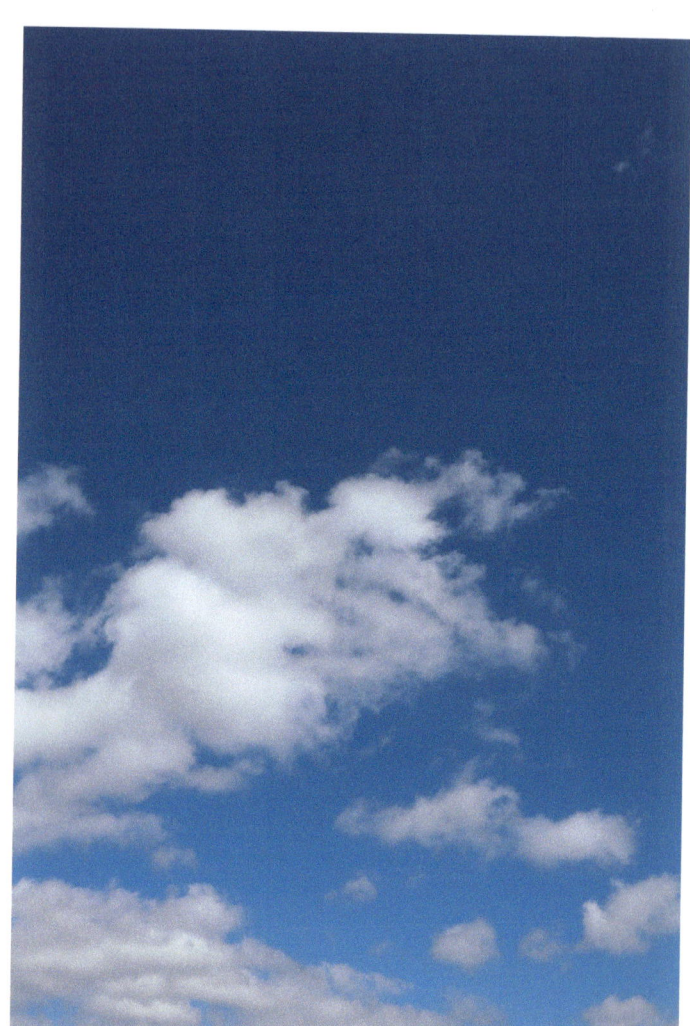

# Cloudy Imaginings

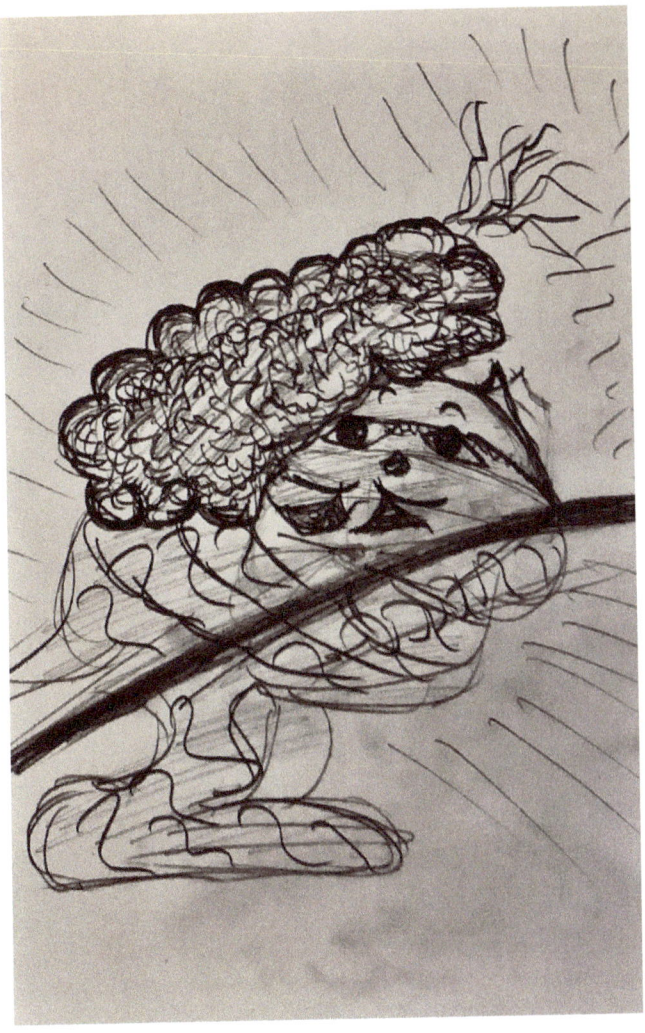

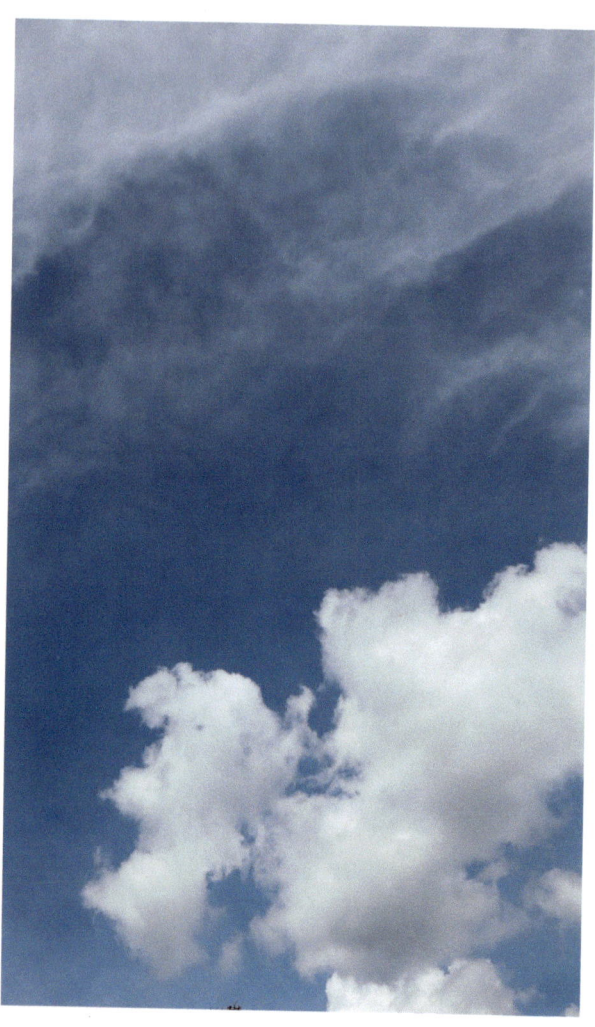

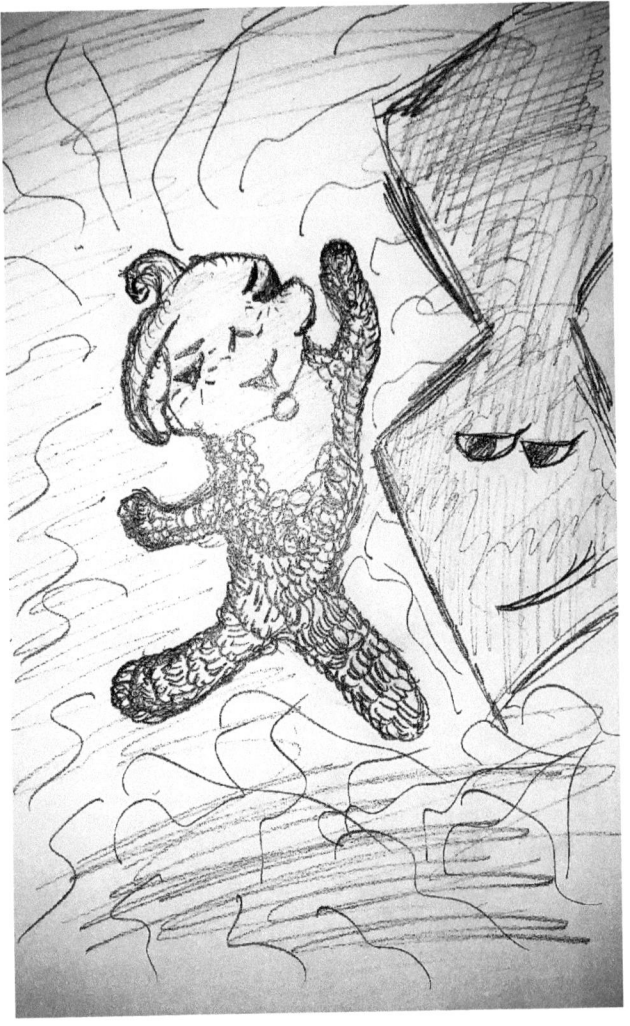

# Cloudy Imaginings

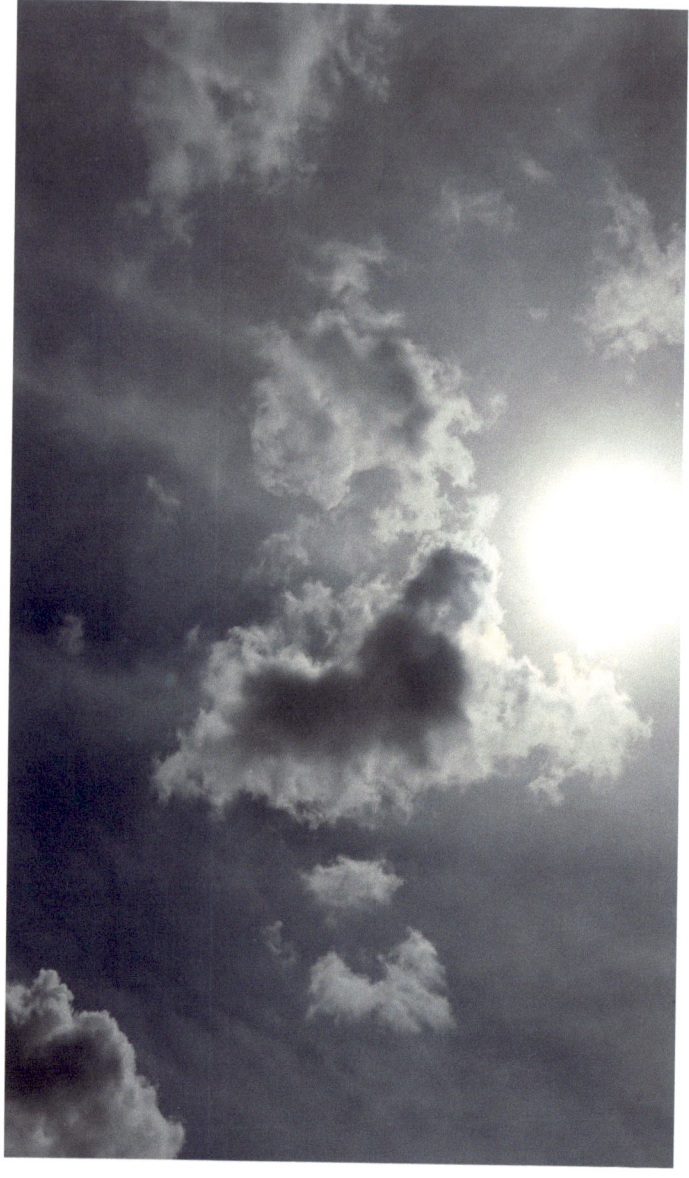

Cloudy Imaginings

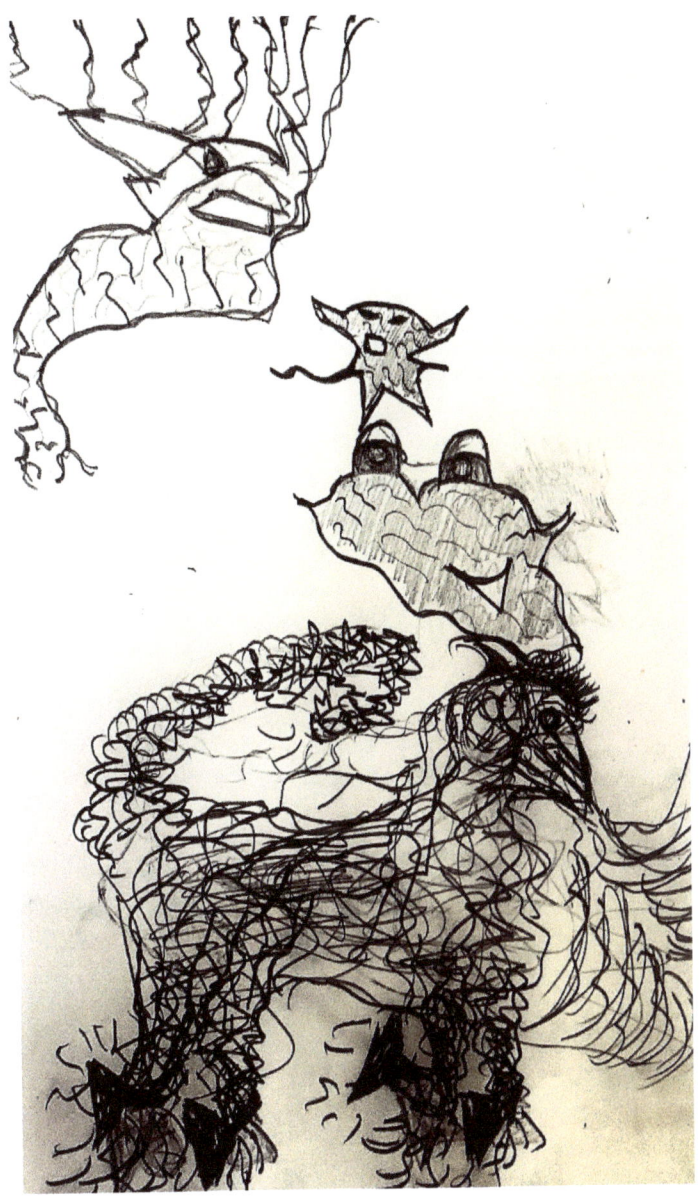

# Cloudy Imaginings

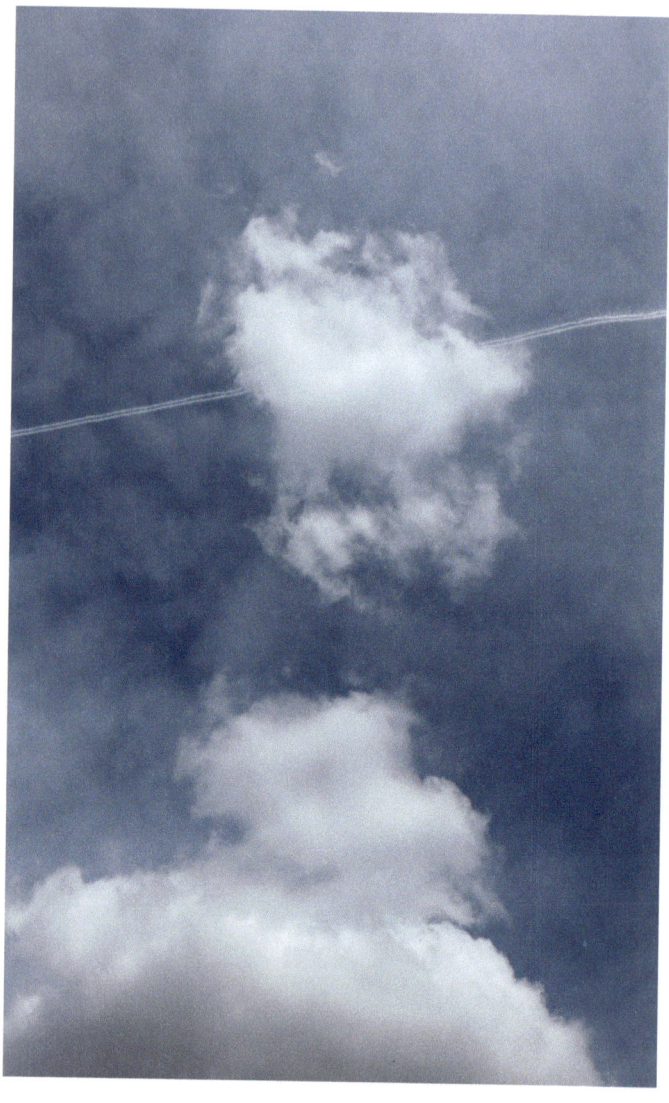

# Cloudy Imaginings

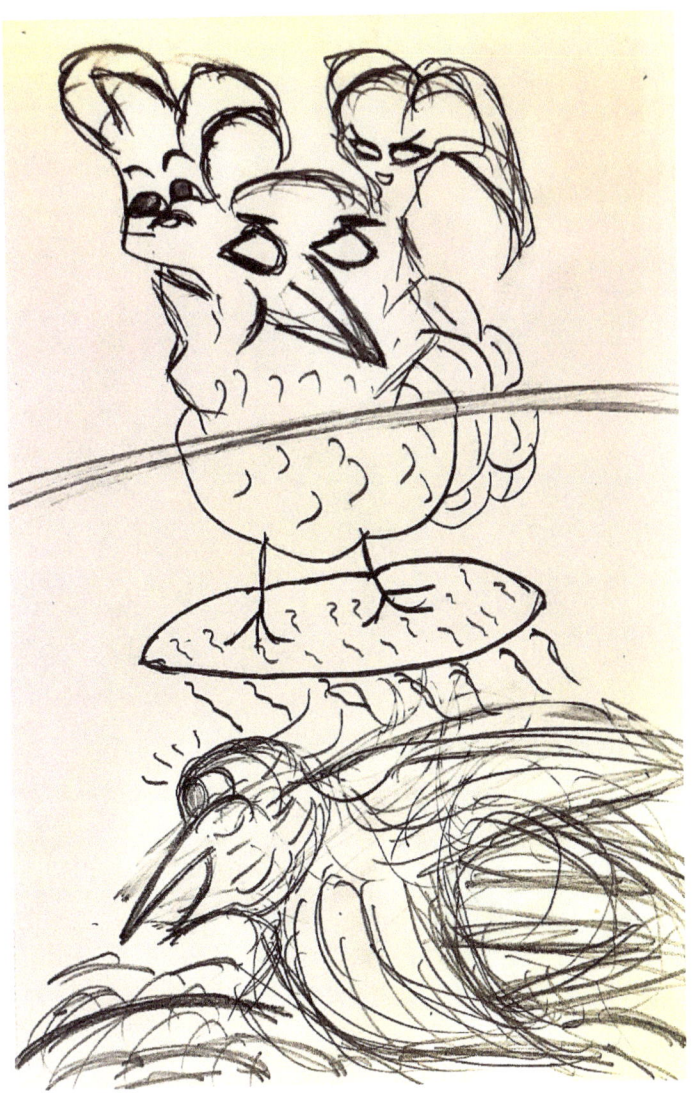

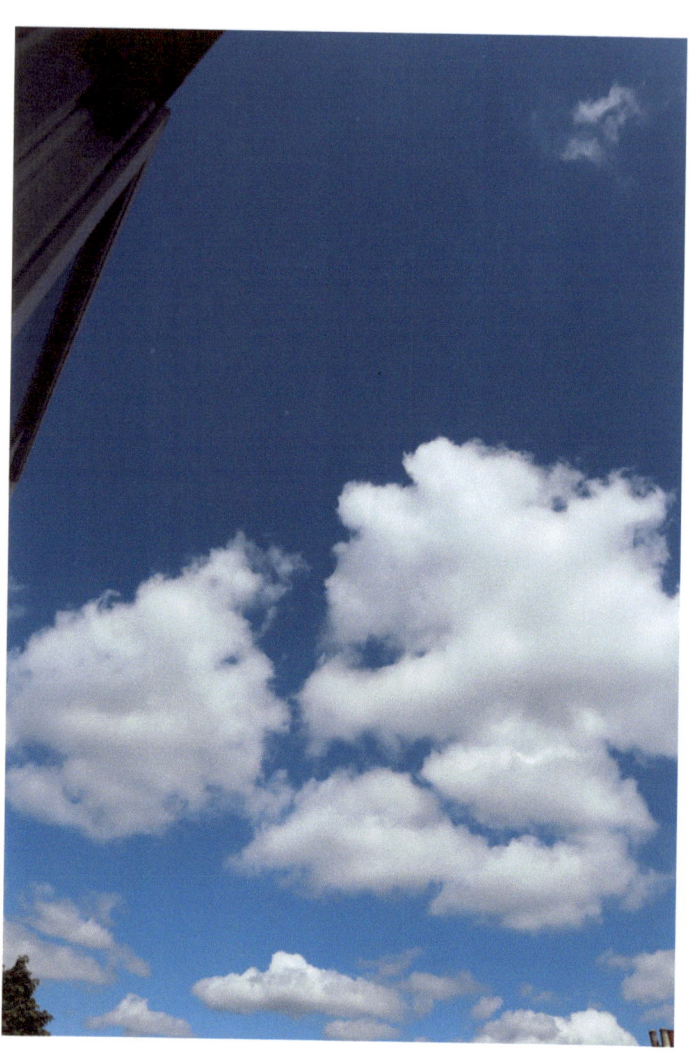

Cloudy Imaginings

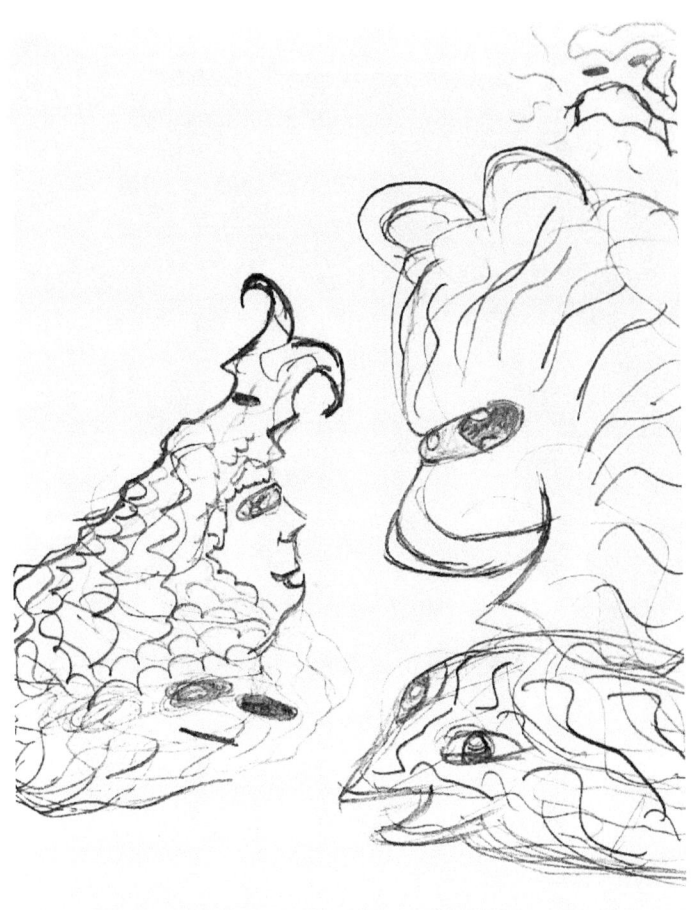

Cloudy Imaginings

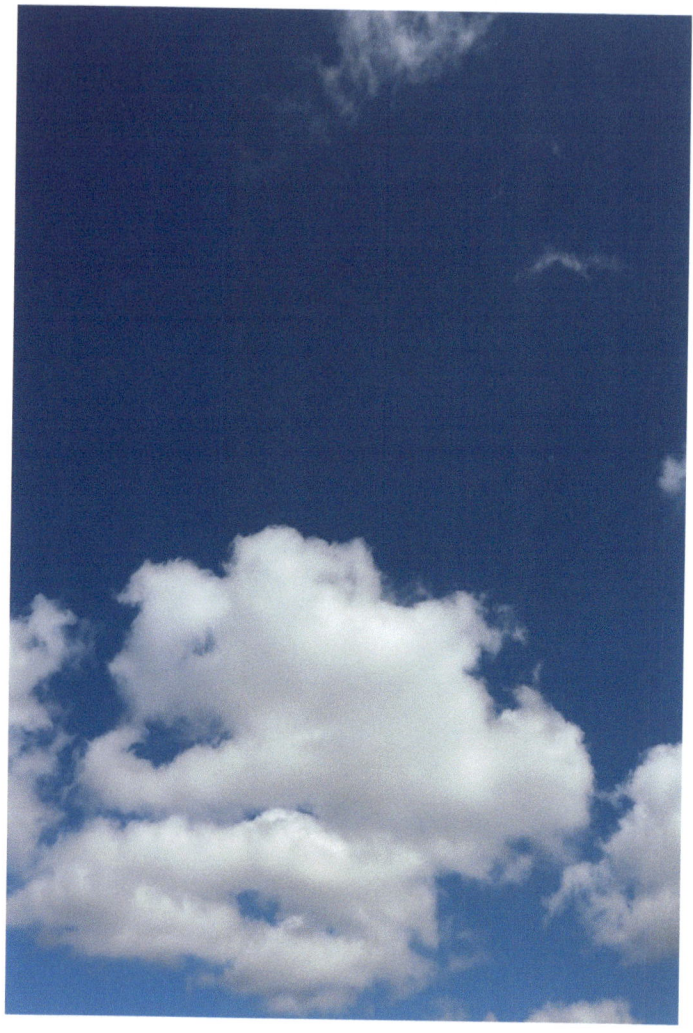

Cloudy Imaginings

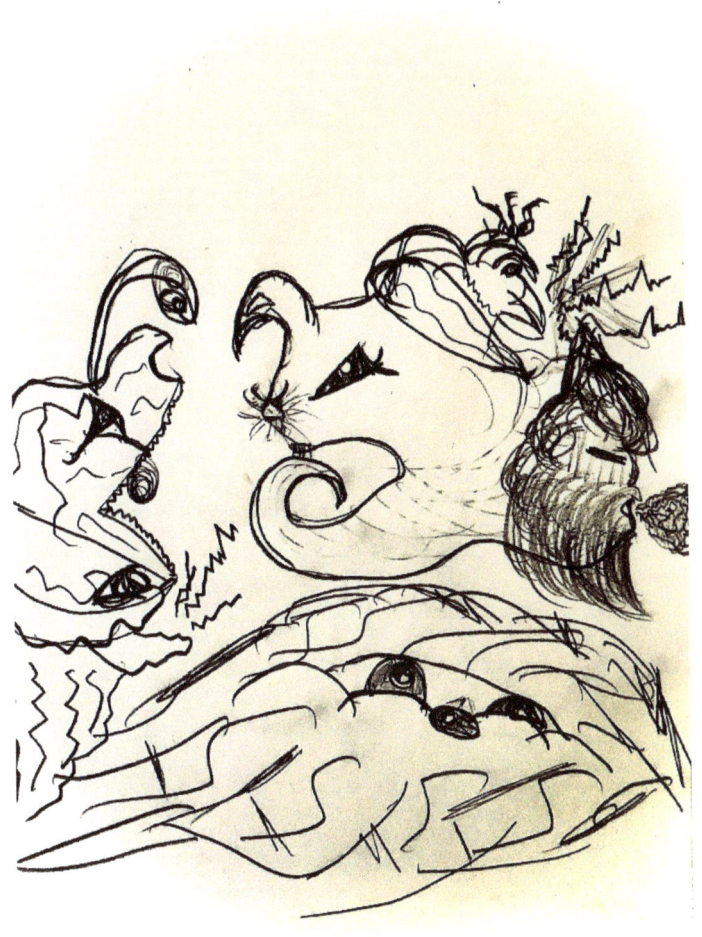

# Cloudy Imaginings

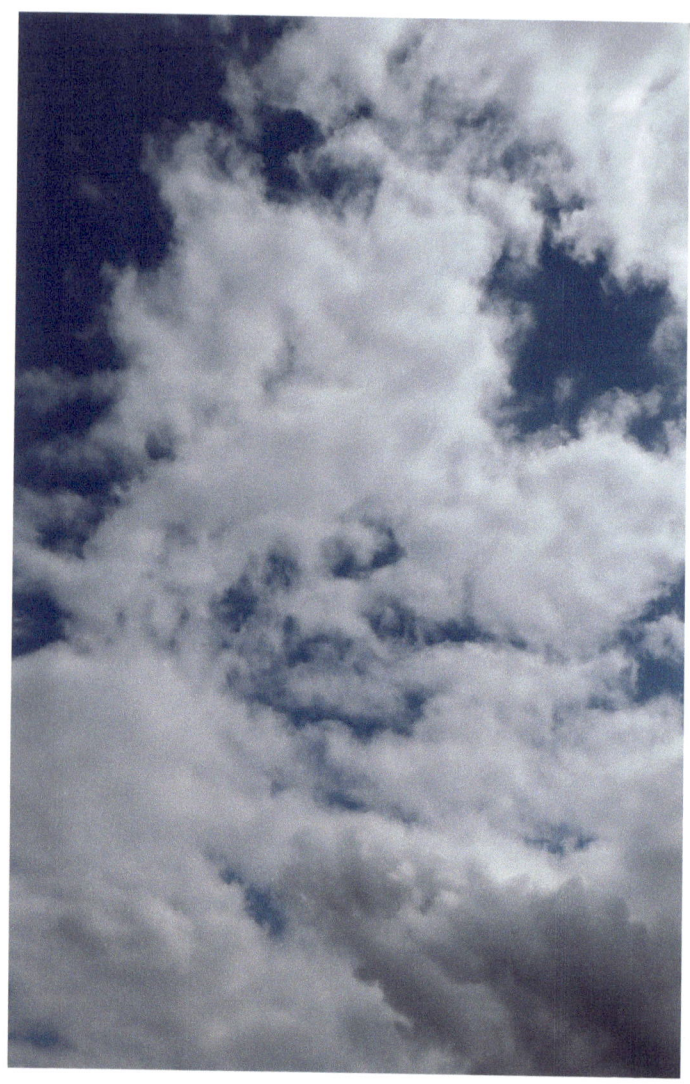

## Cloudy Imaginings

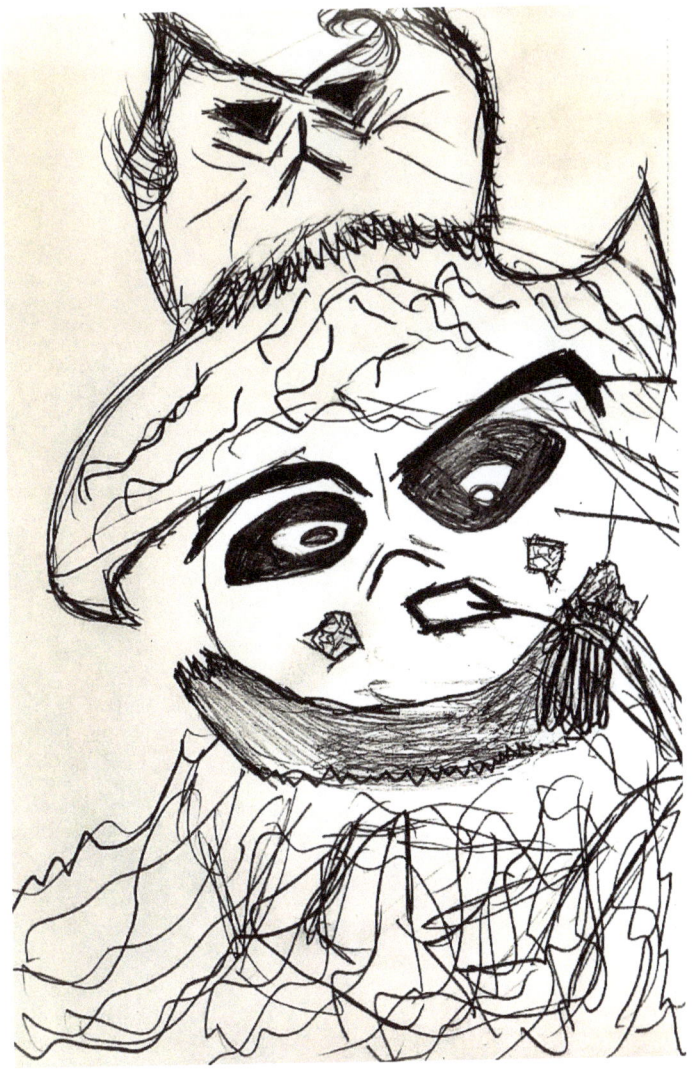

# Cloudy Imaginings

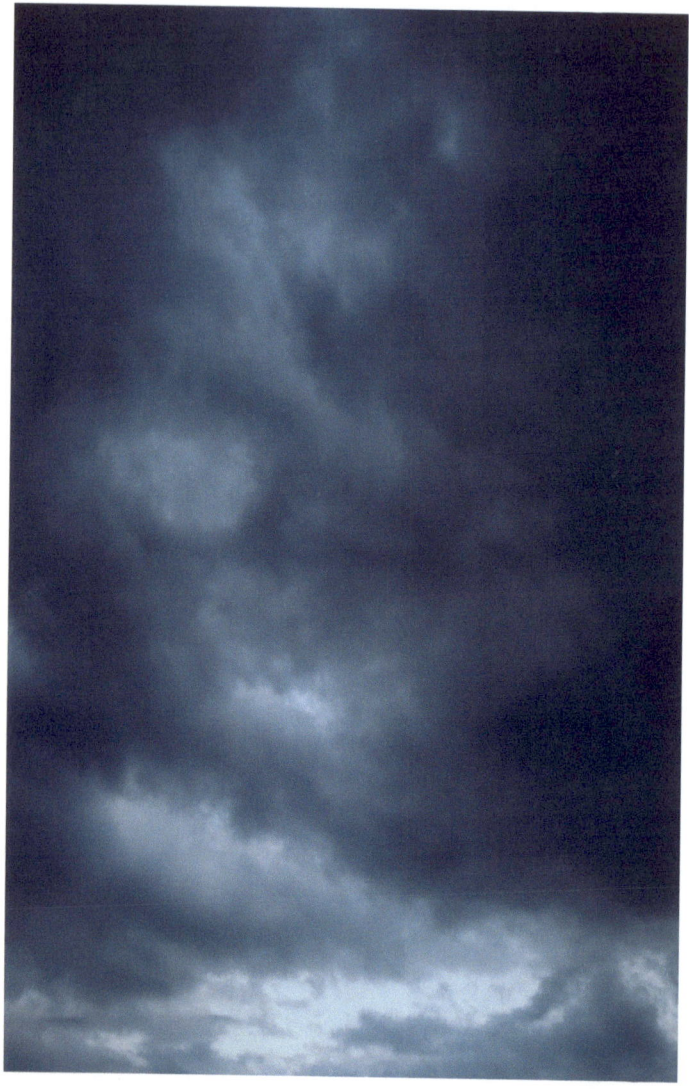

Cloudy Imaginings

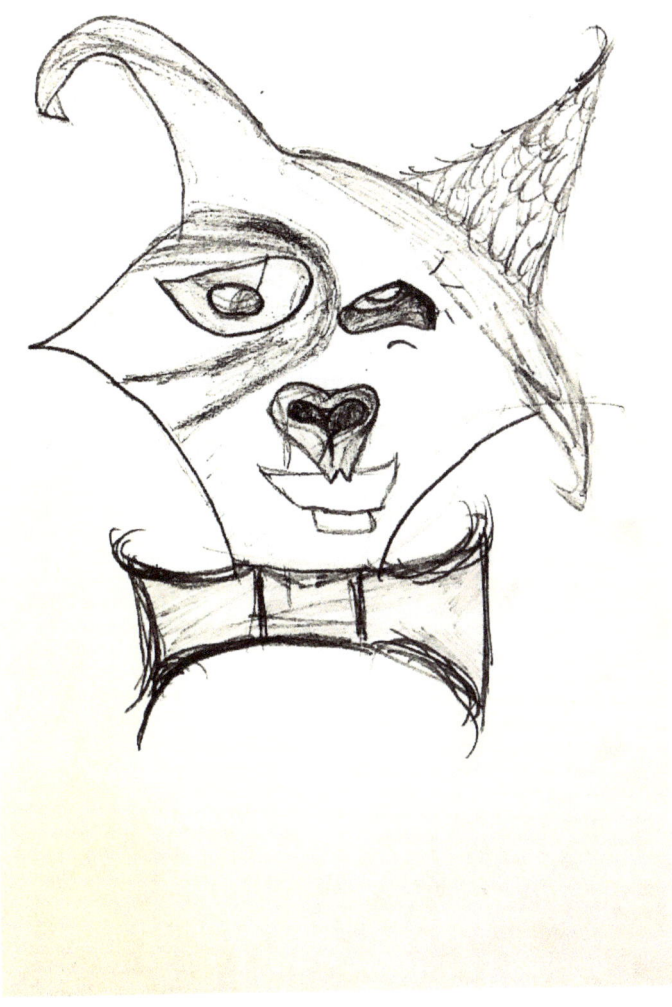

Cloudy Imaginings

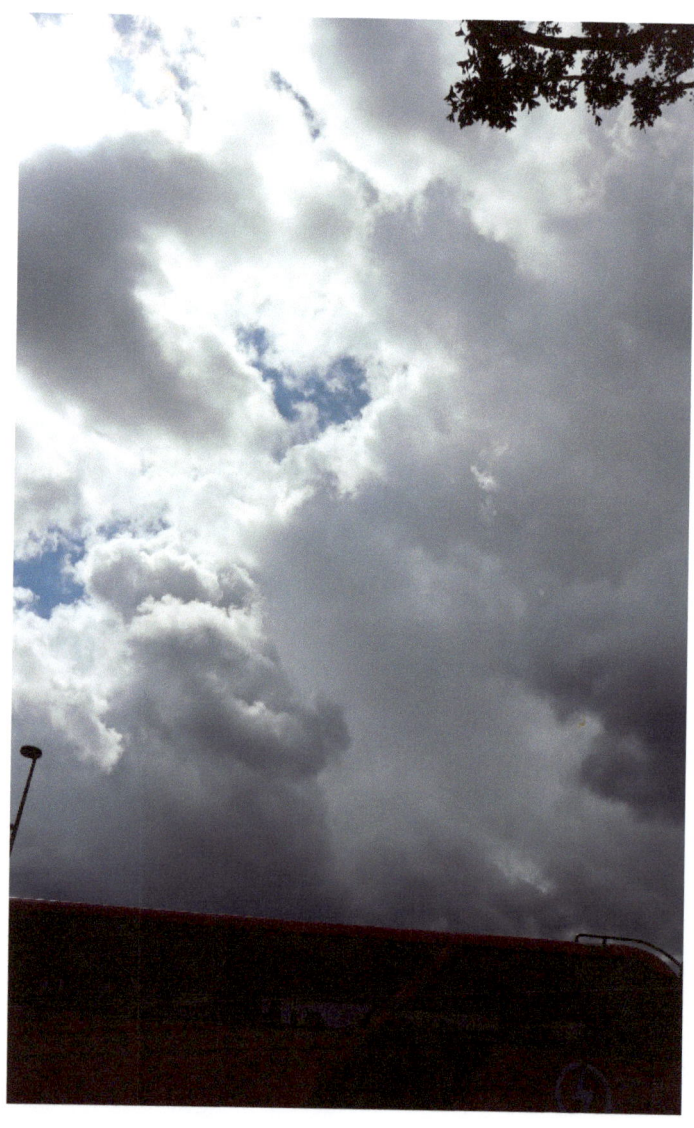

Cloudy Imaginings

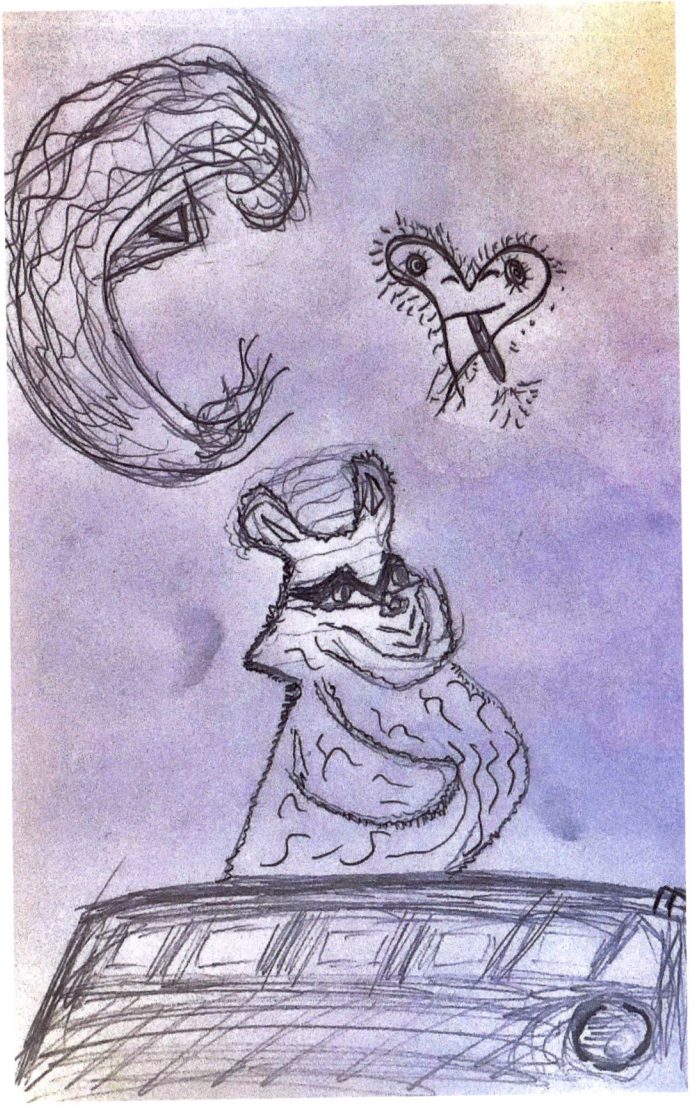

Cloudy Imaginings

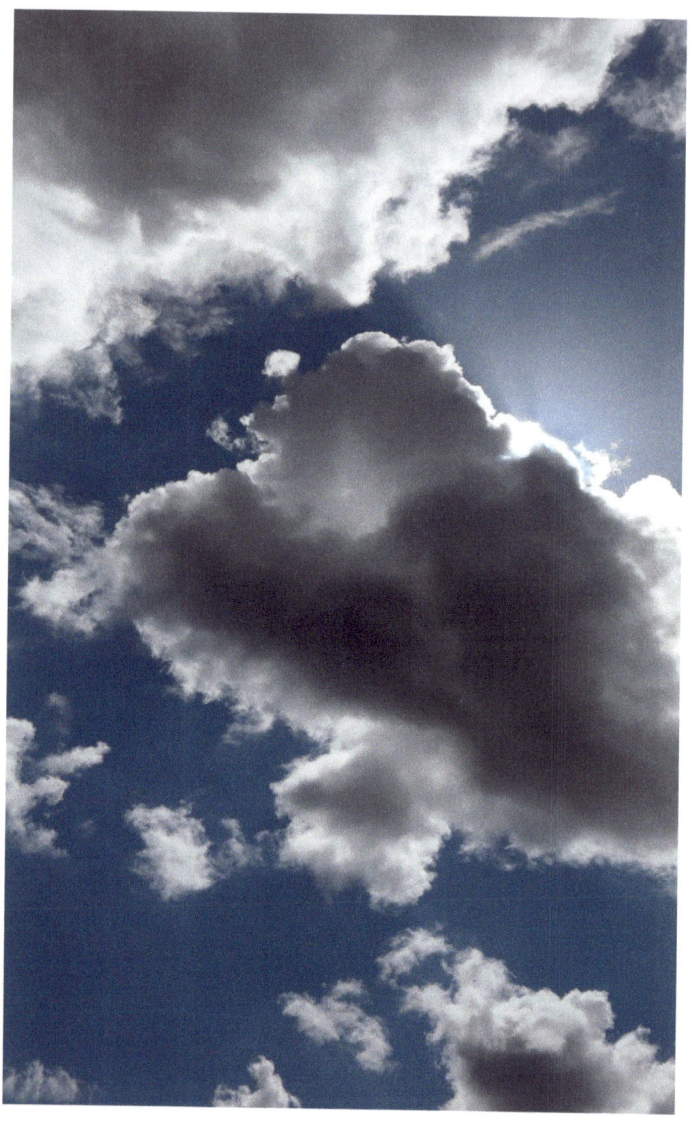

Cloudy Imaginings

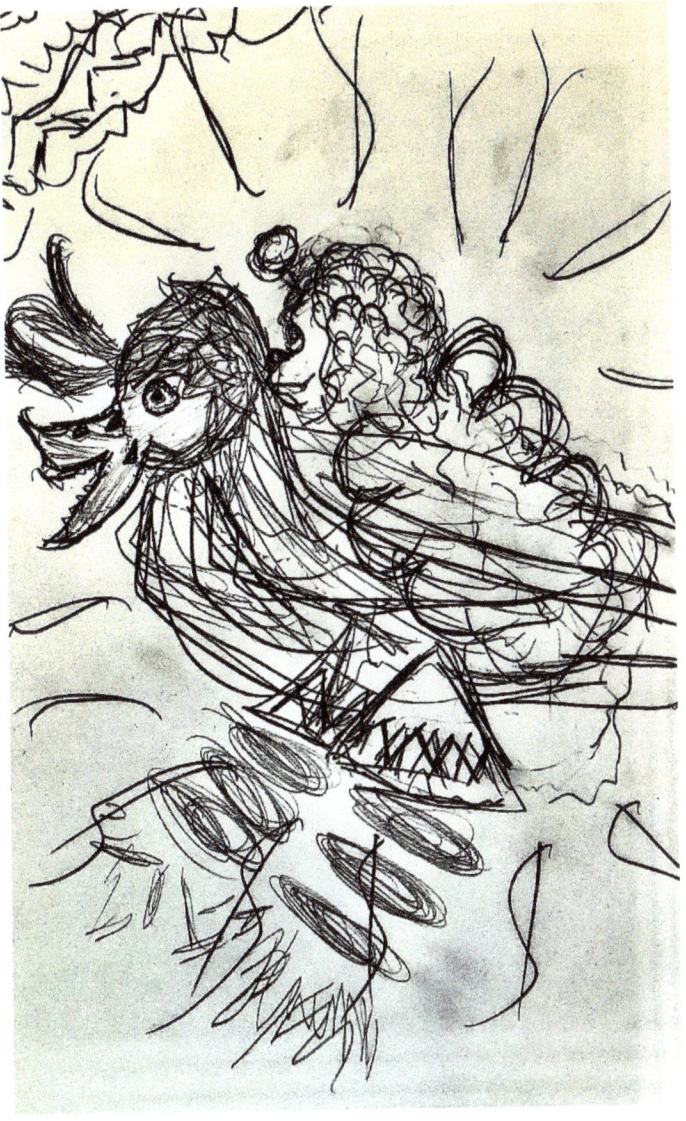

# Cloudy Imaginings

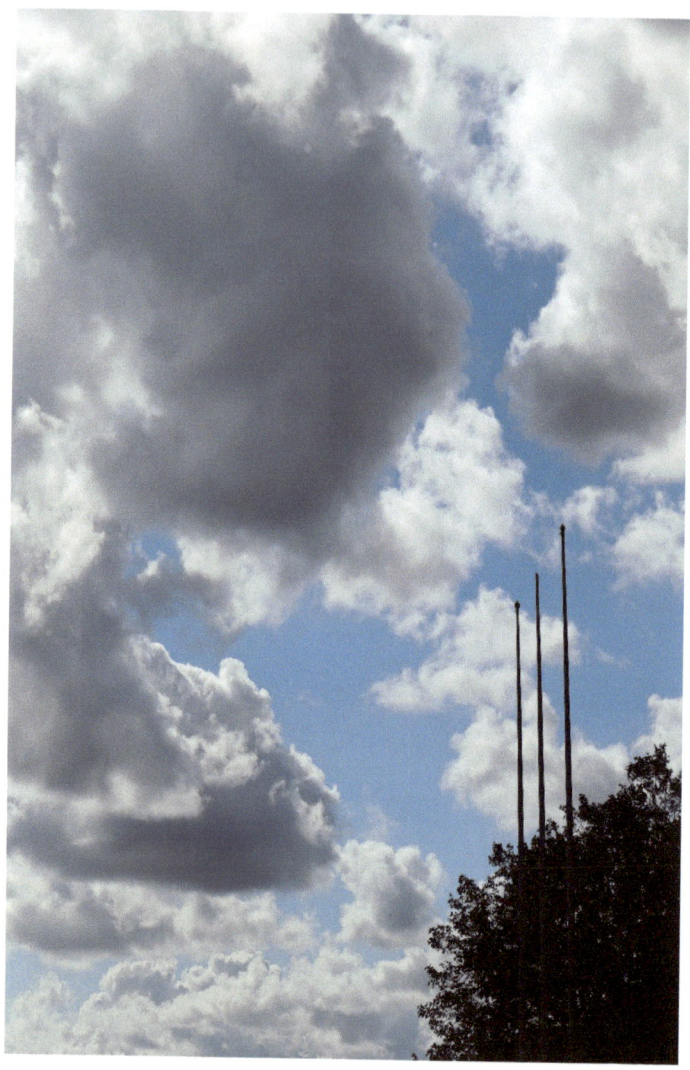

# Cloudy Imaginings

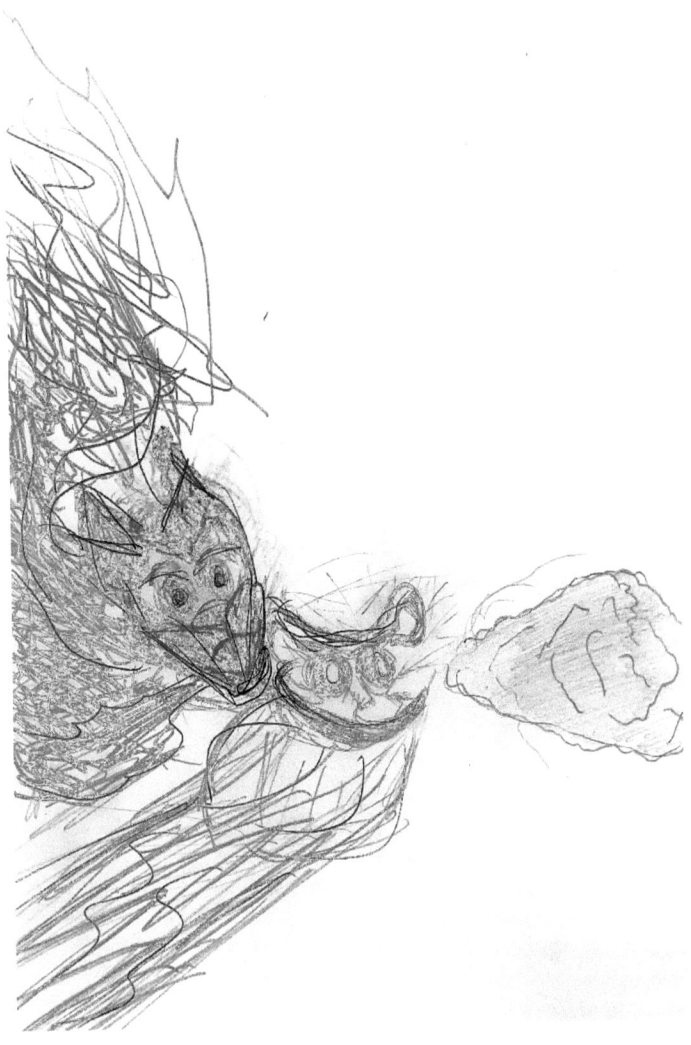

# Cloudy Imaginings

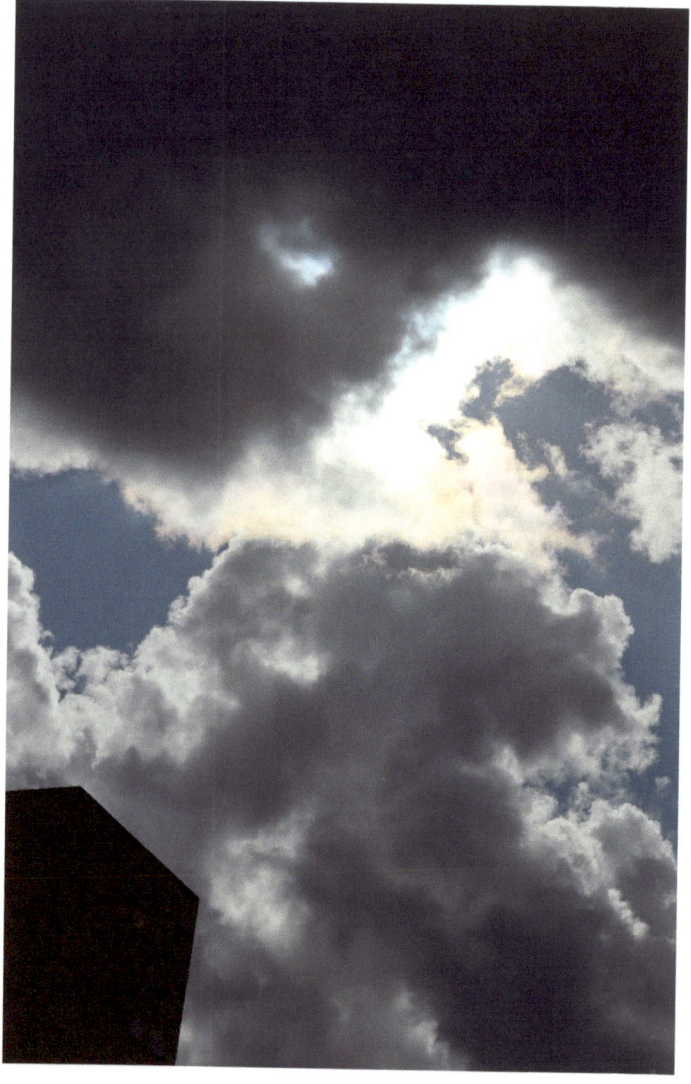

Cloudy Imaginings

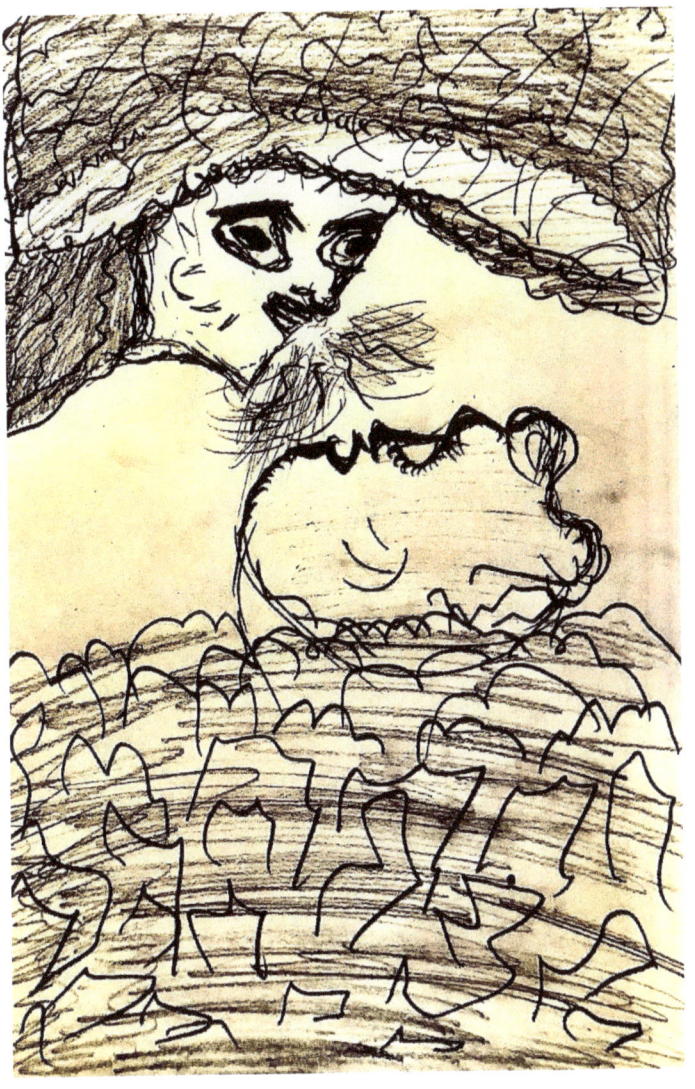

Cloudy Imaginings

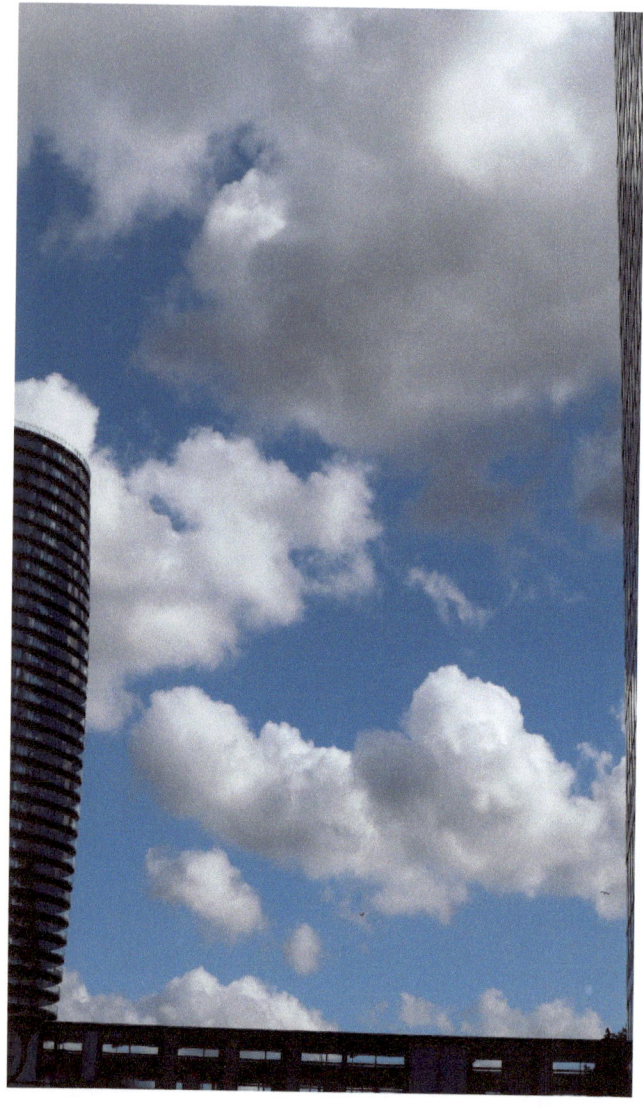

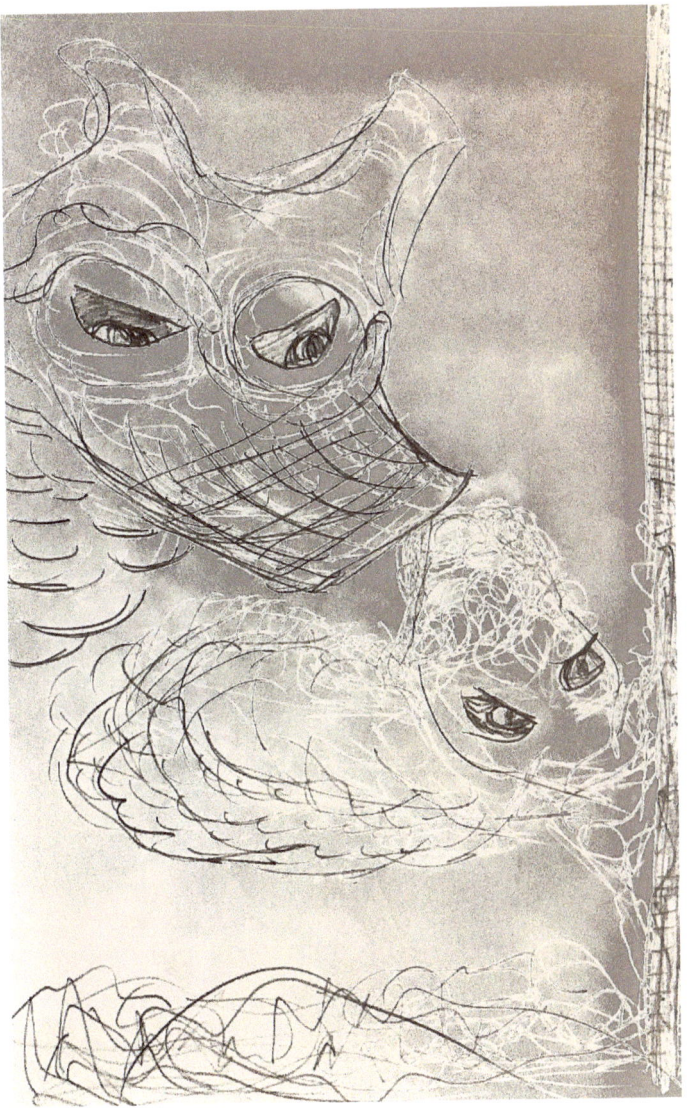

Cloudy Imaginings

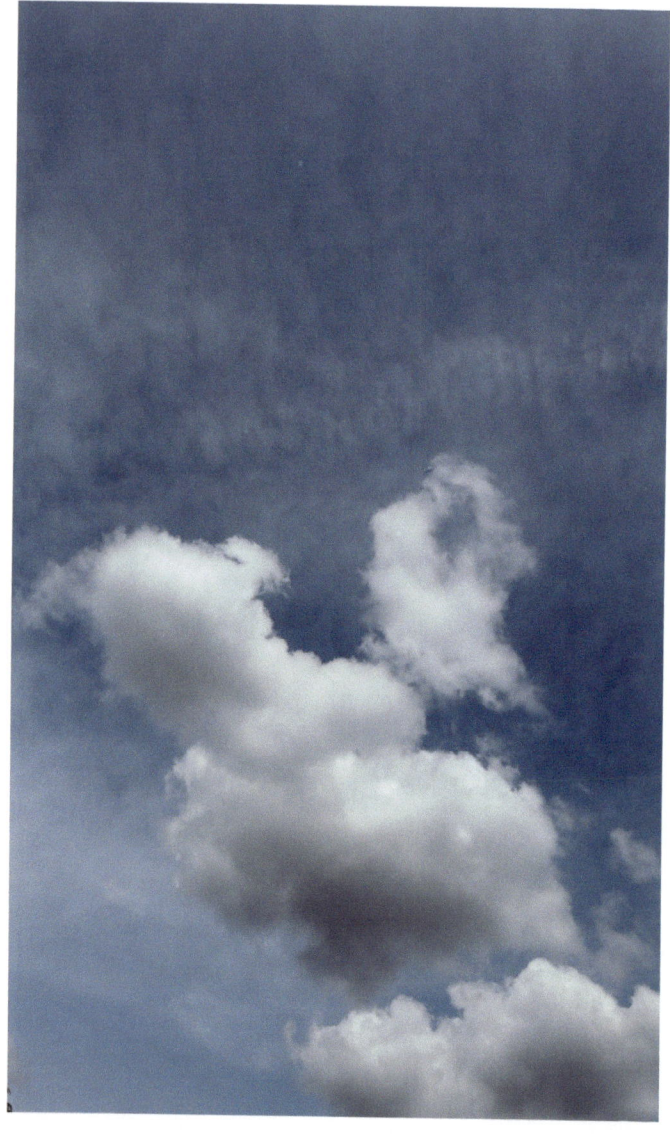

# Cloudy Imaginings

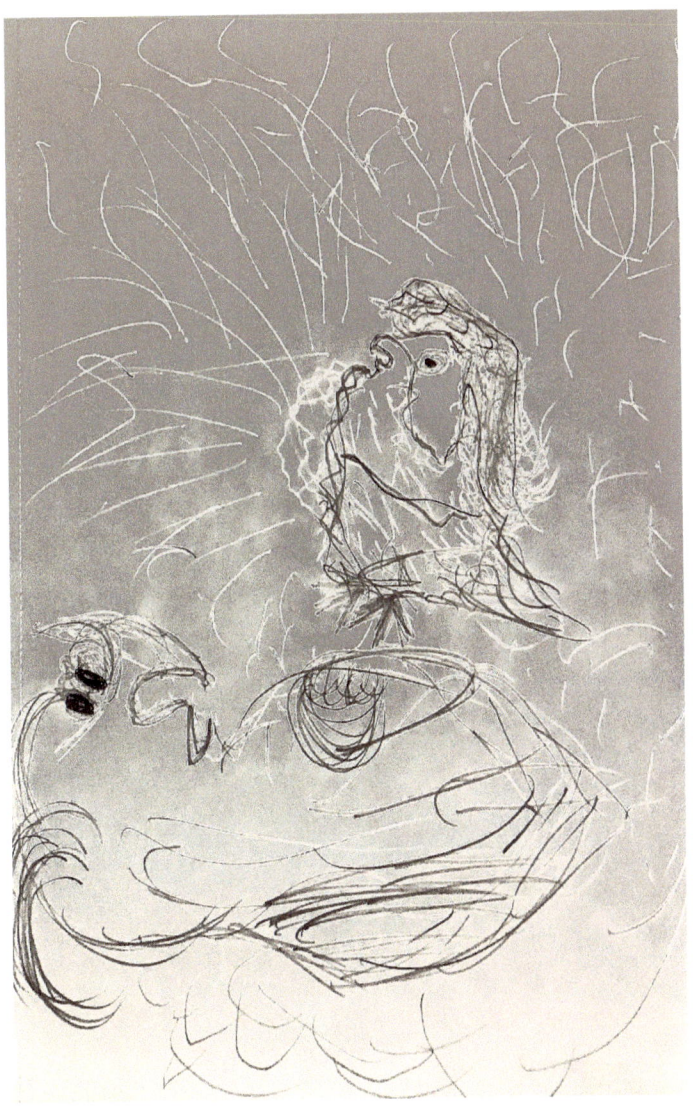

Cloudy Imaginings

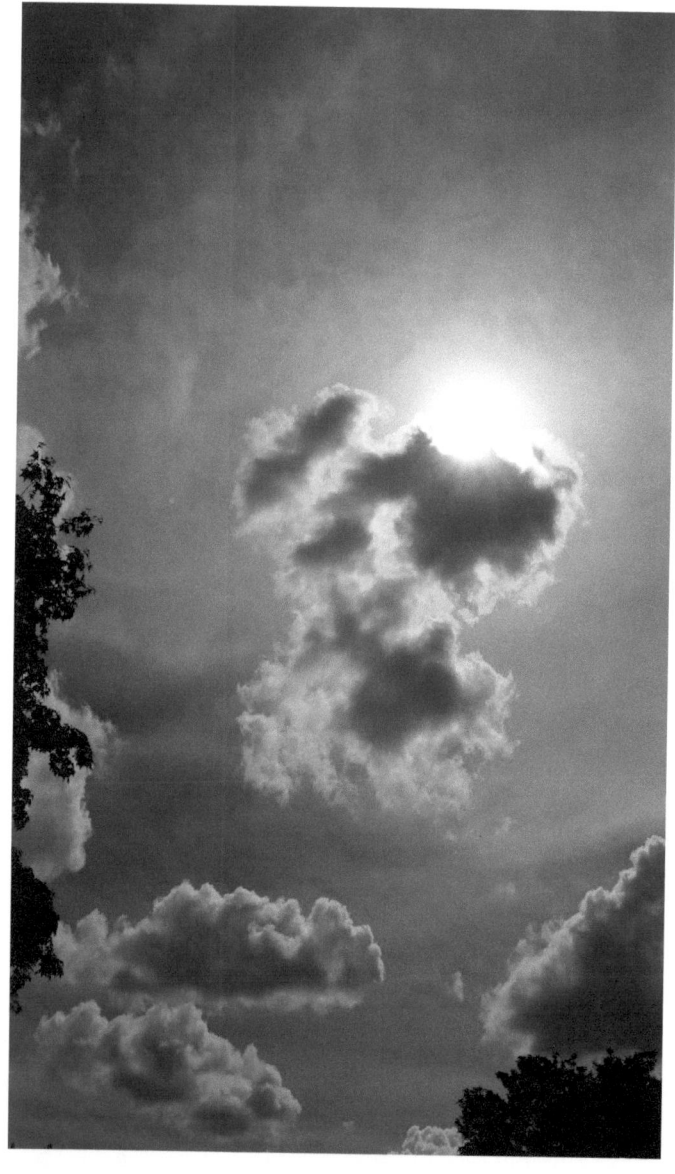

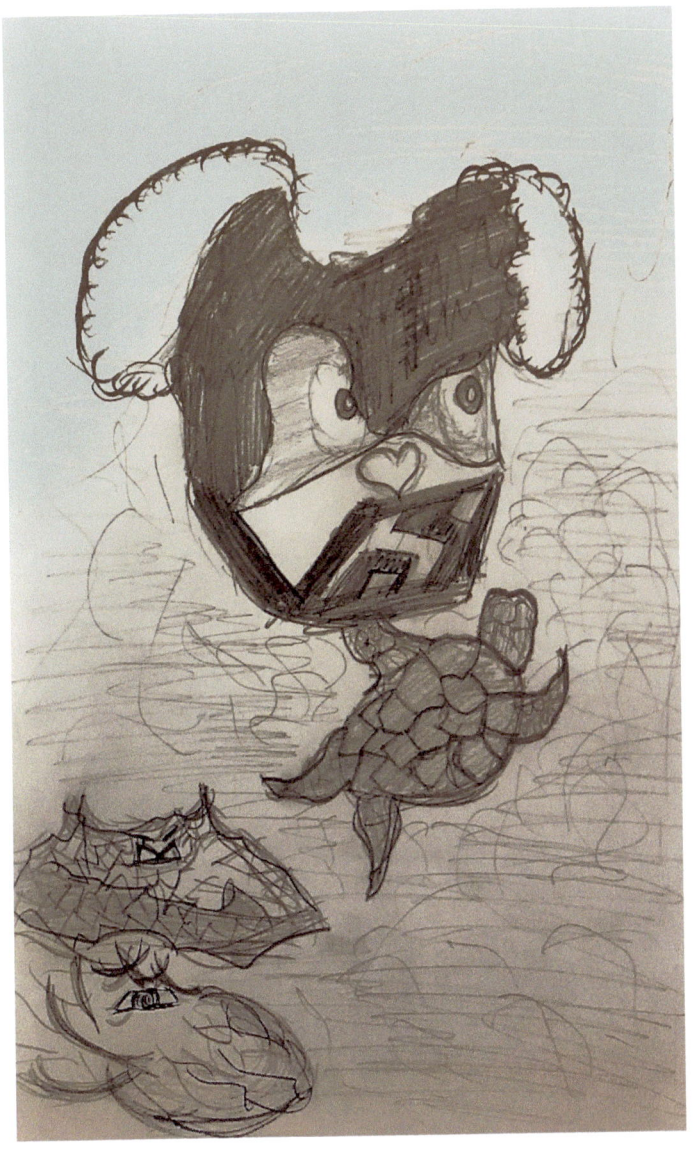

Cloudy Imaginings

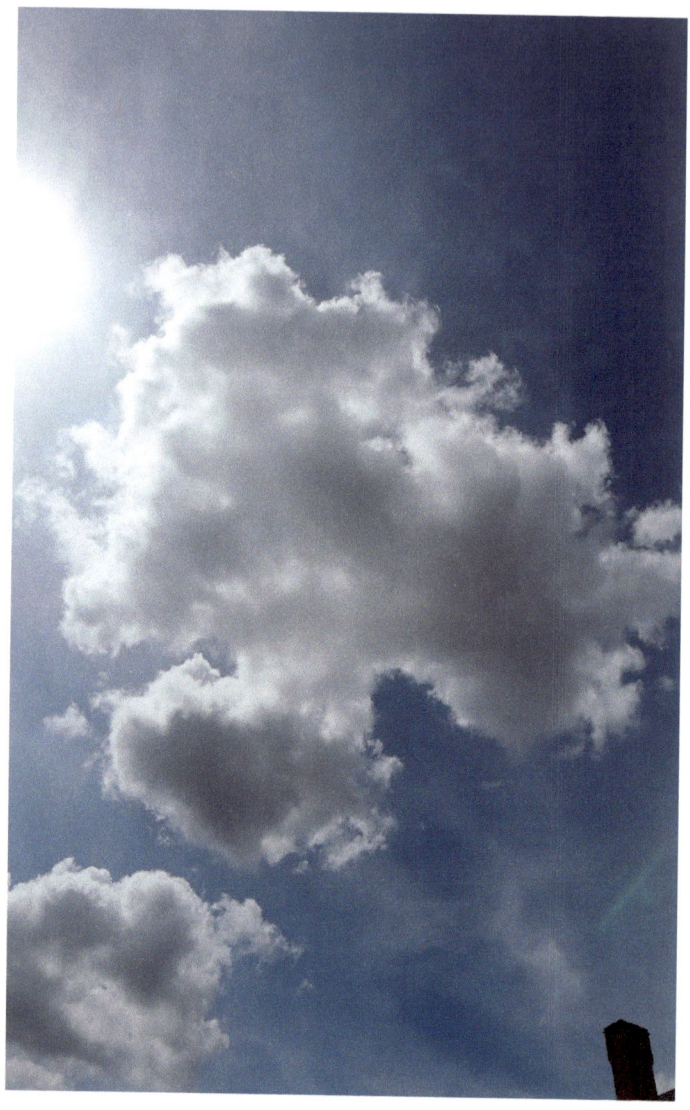

# Cloudy Imaginings

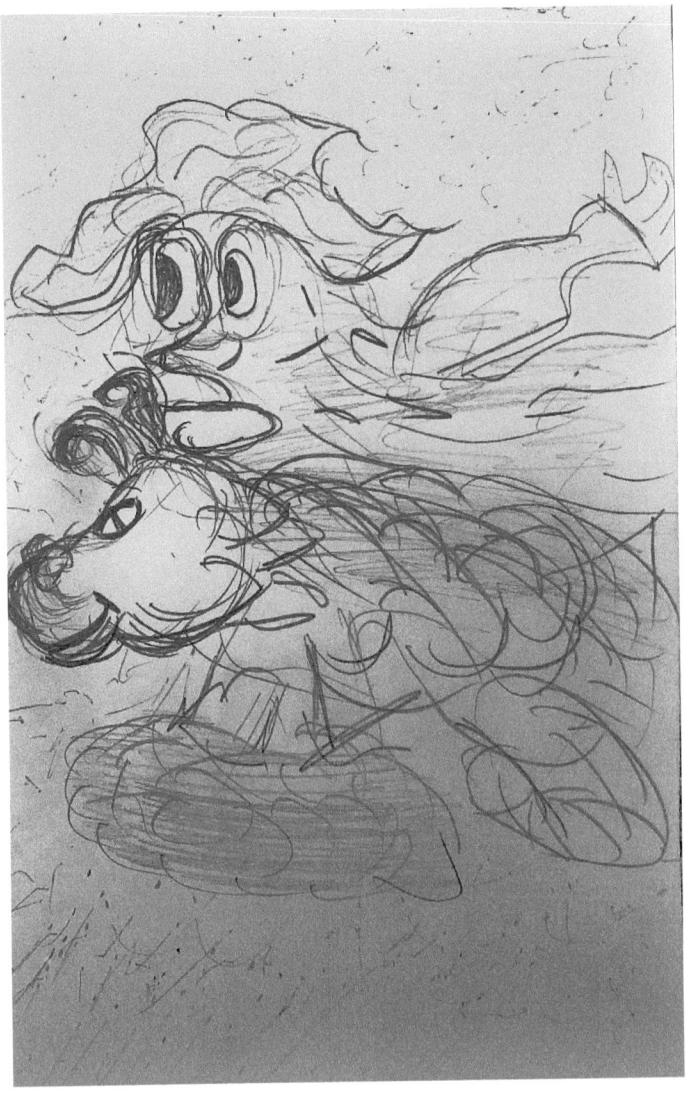

# Cloudy Imaginings

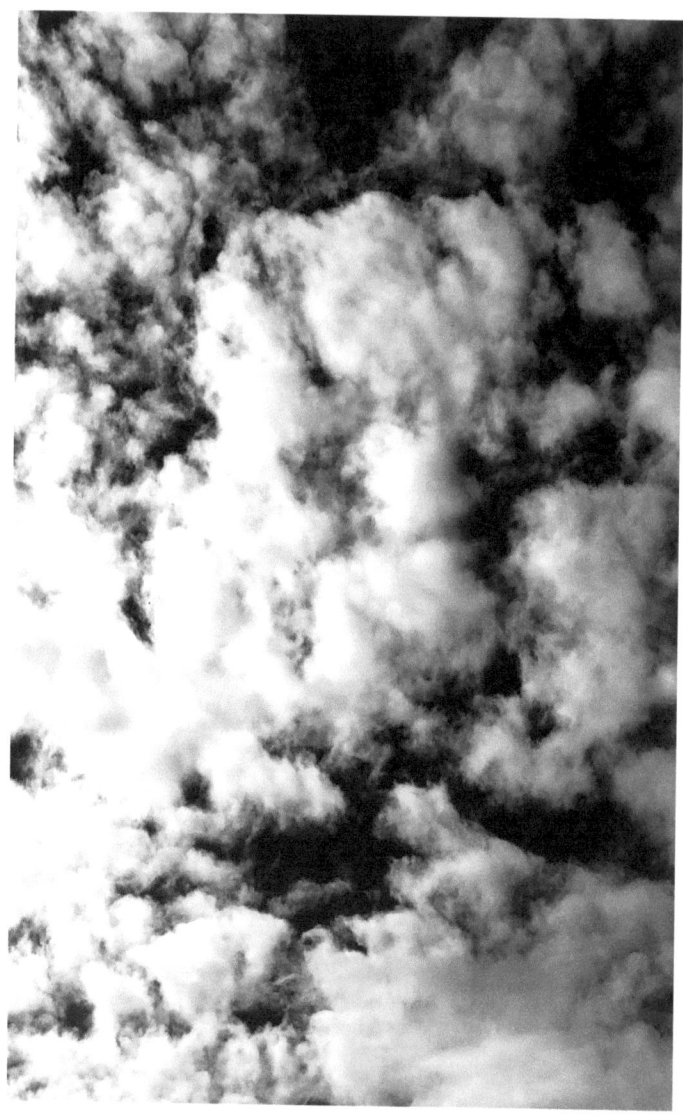

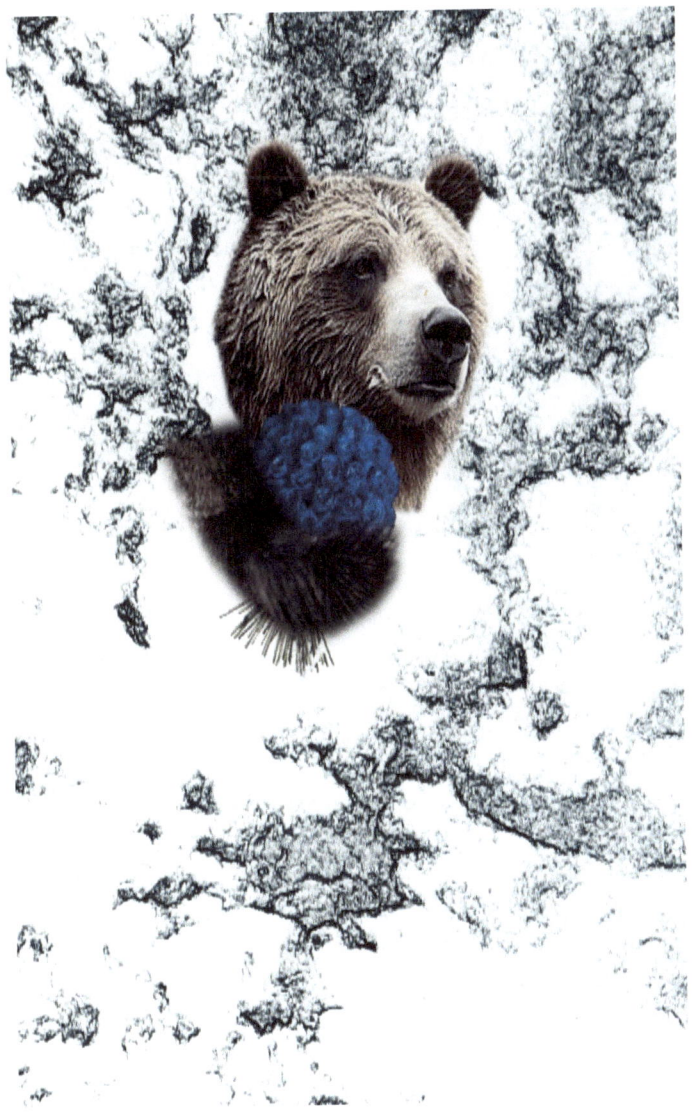

# Cloudy Imaginings

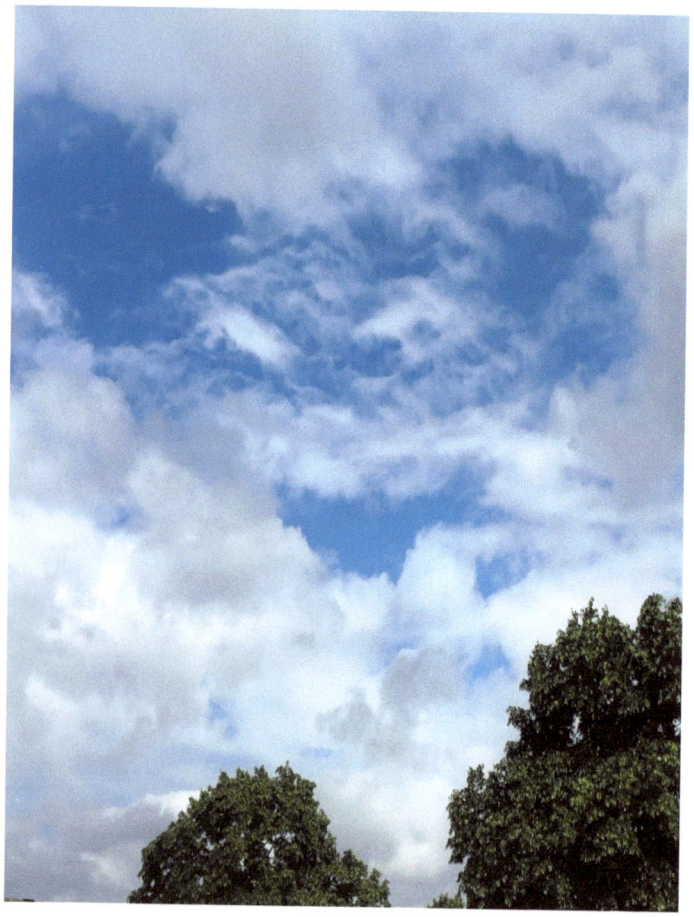

Cloudy Imaginings

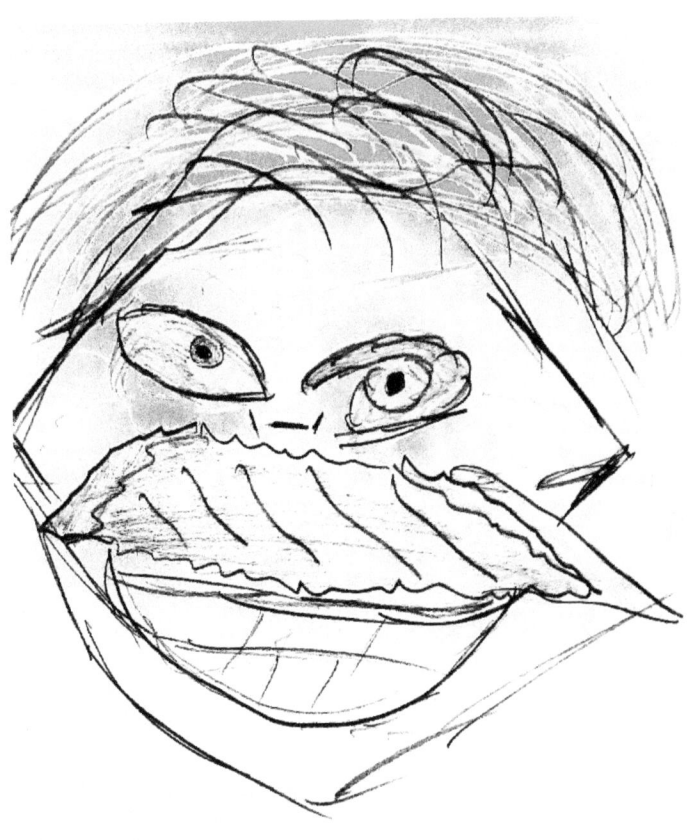

# Cloudy Imaginings

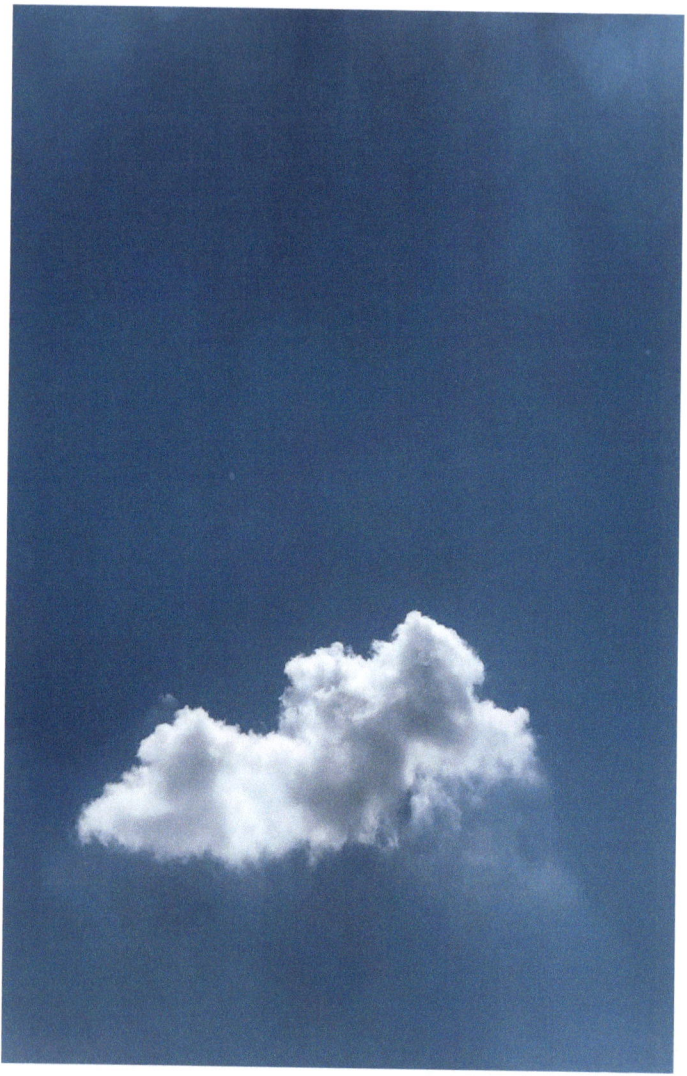

# Cloudy Imaginings

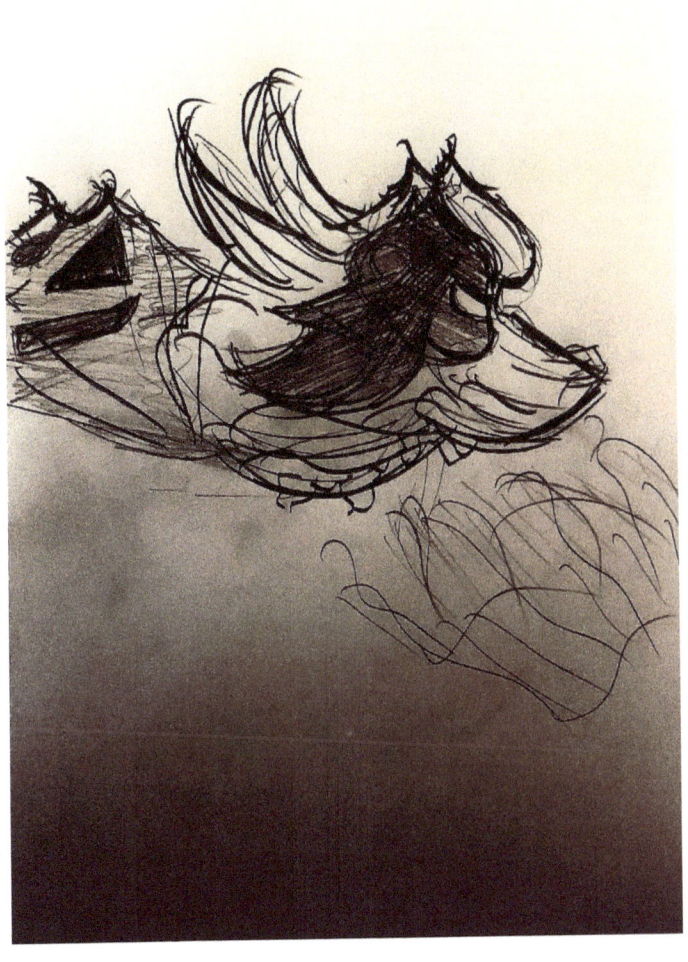

# Cloudy Imaginings

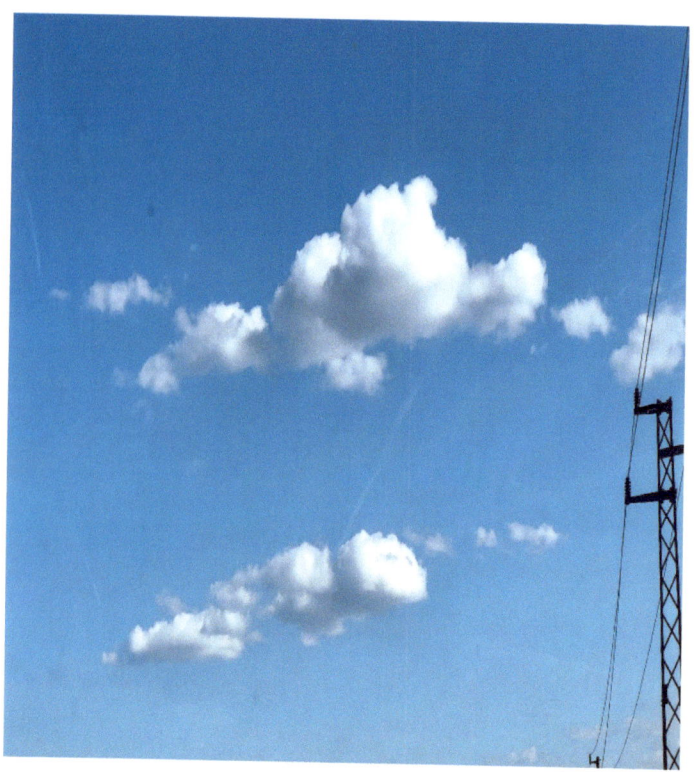

# Cloudy Imaginings

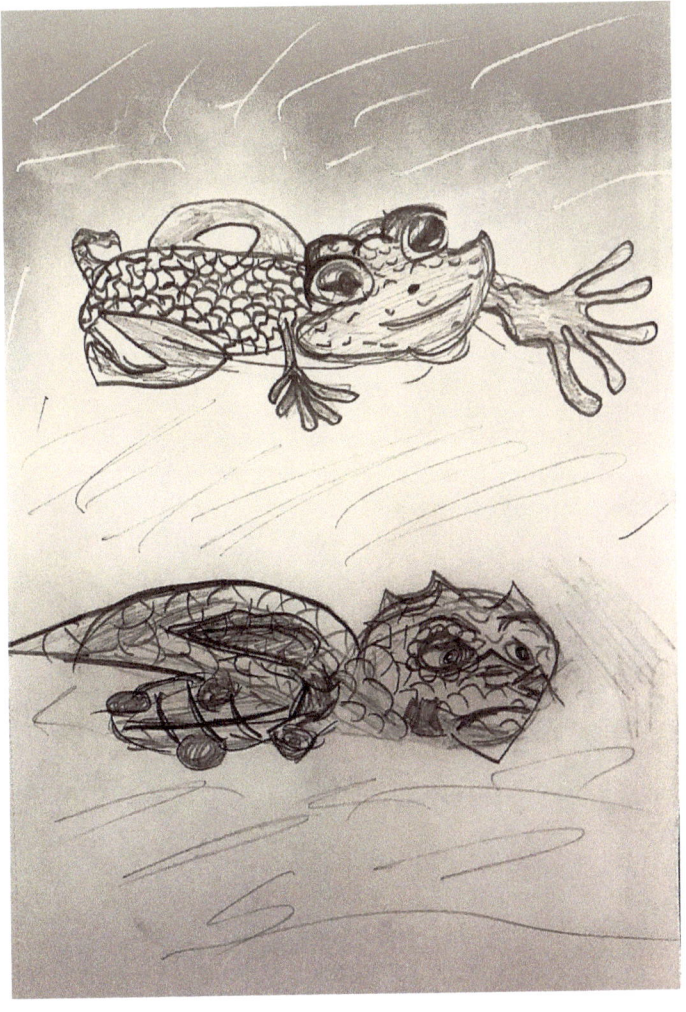

Cloudy Imaginings

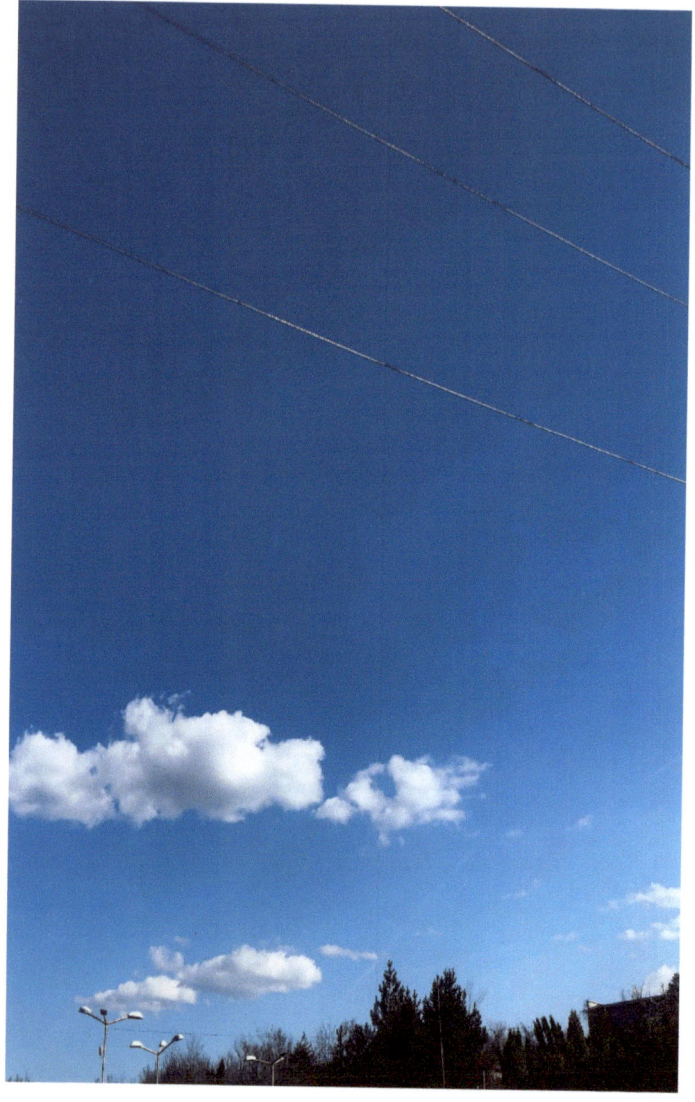

Cloudy Imaginings

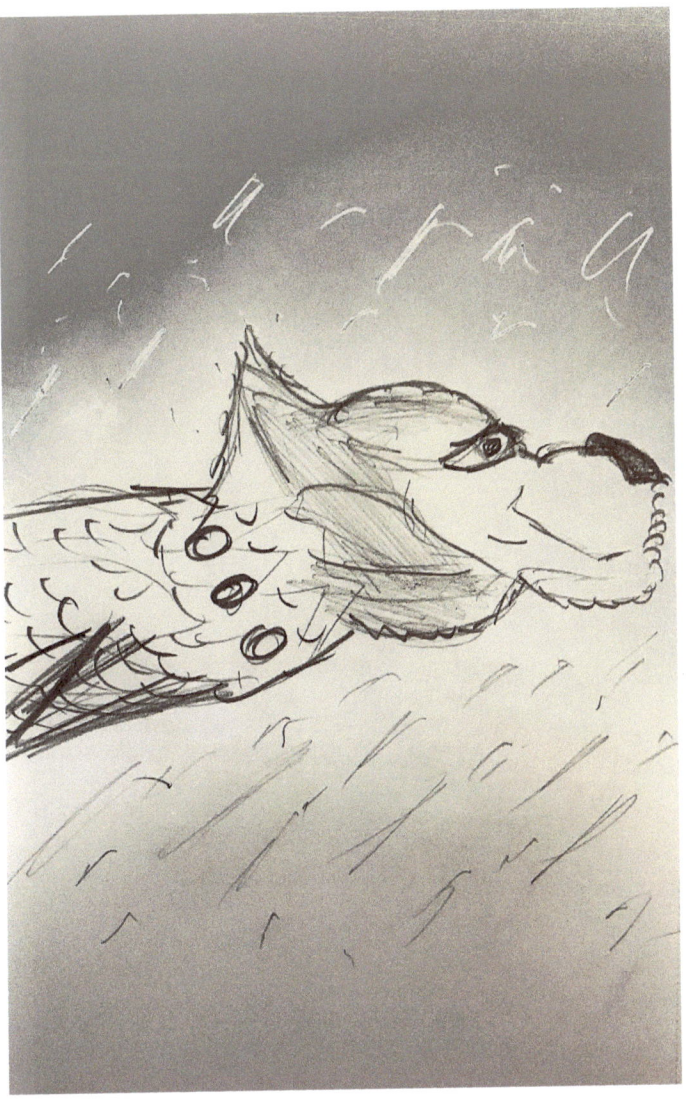

# Cloudy Imaginings

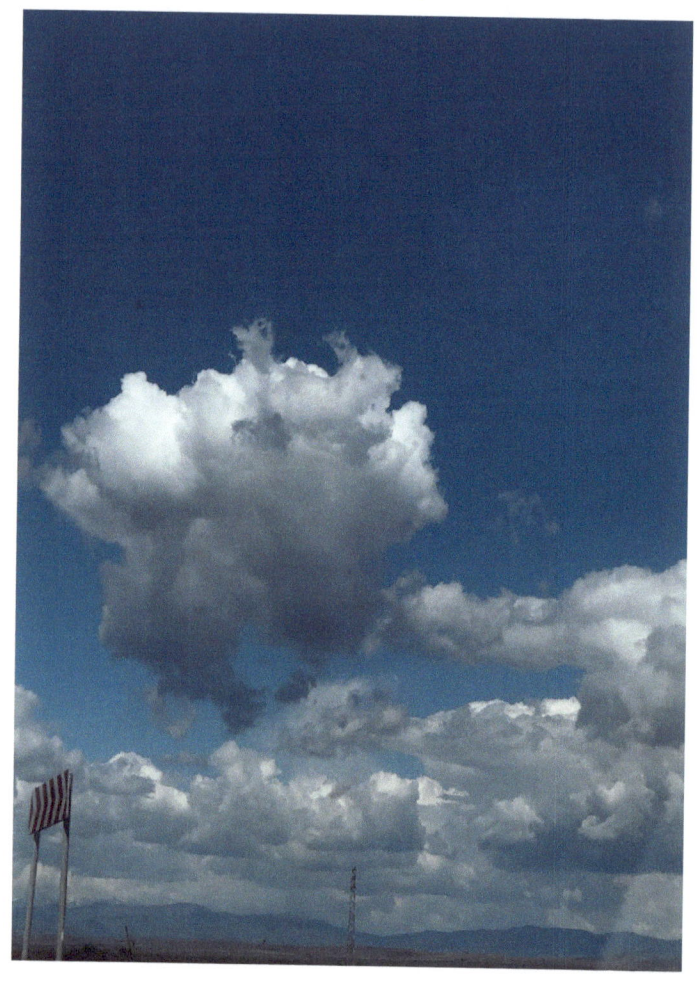

Cloudy Imaginings

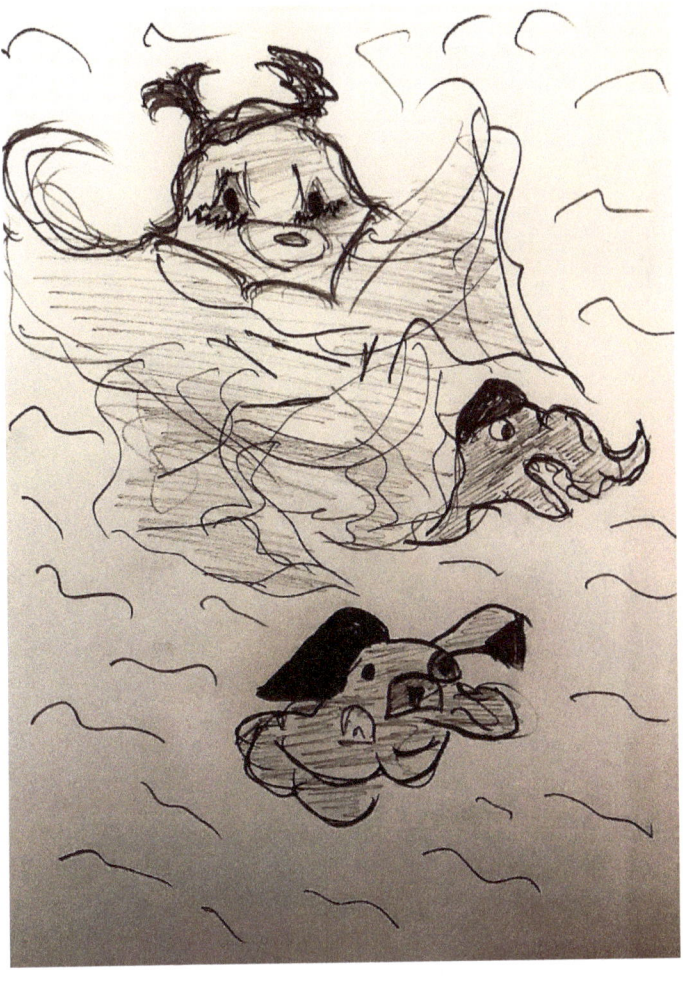

# Cloudy Imaginings

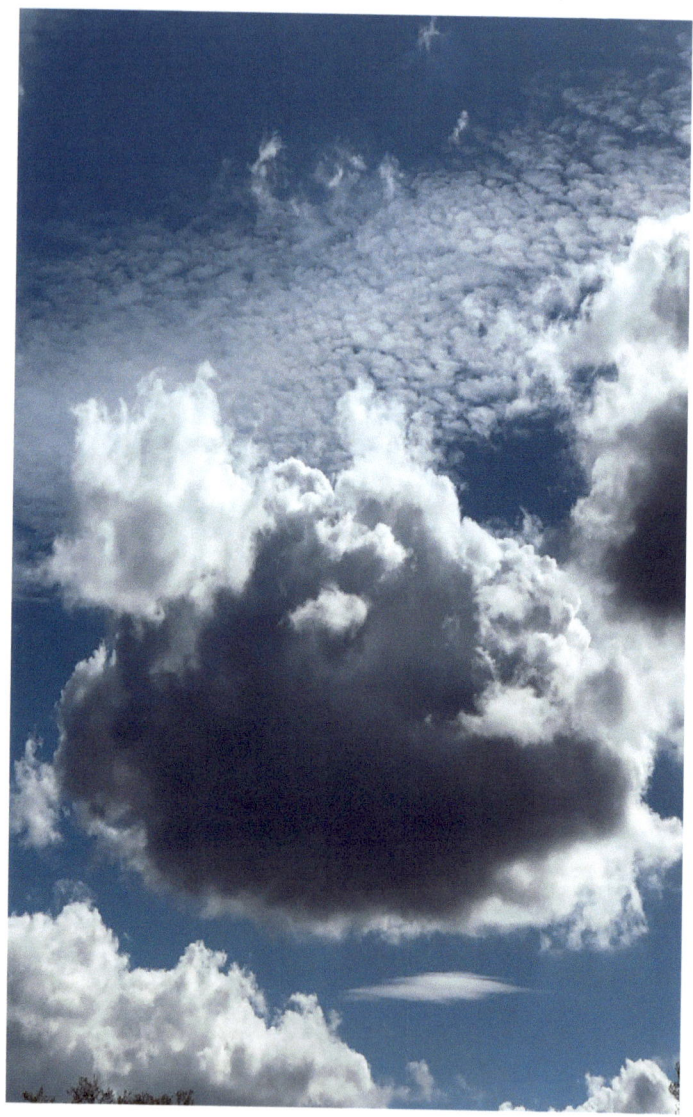

Cloudy Imaginings

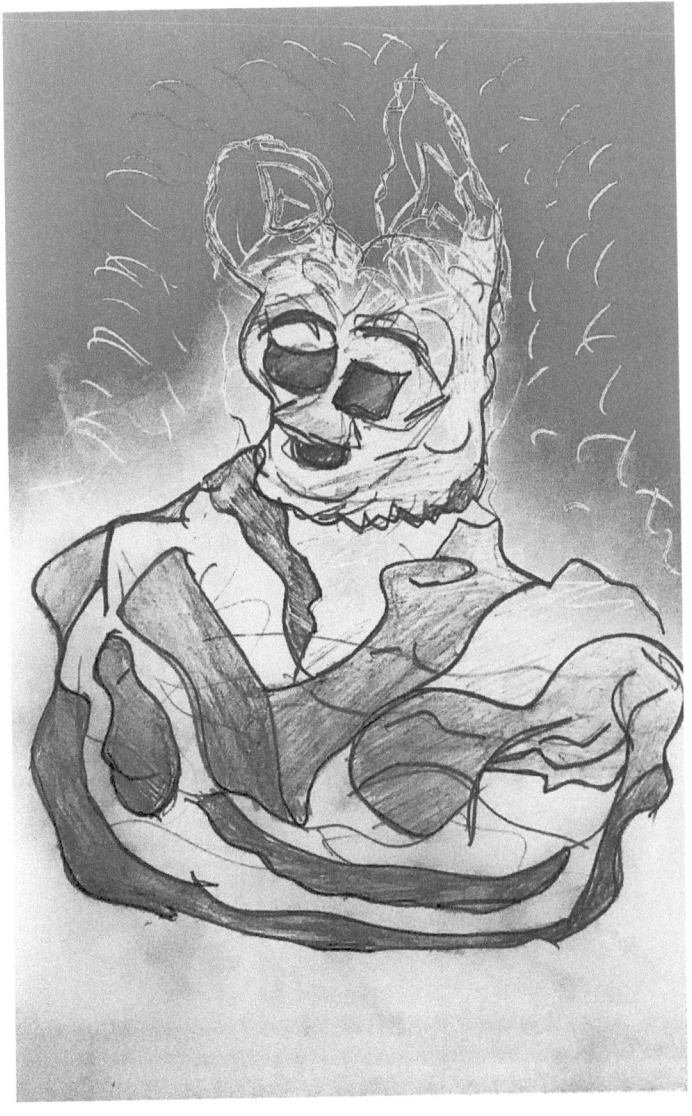

Cloudy Imaginings

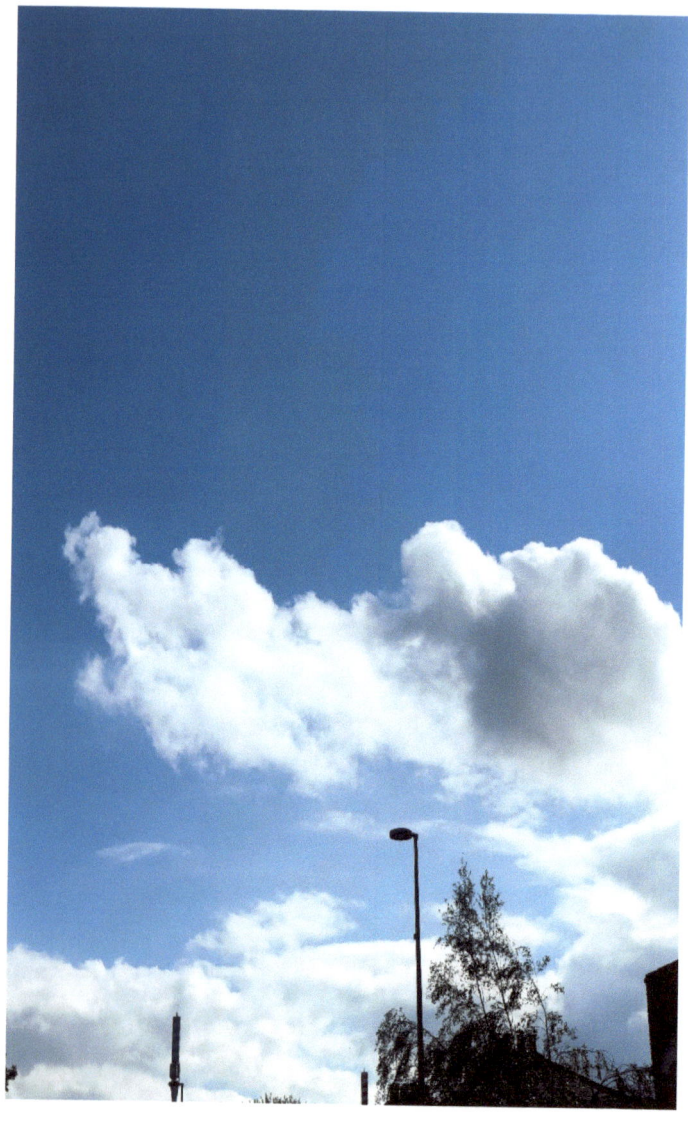

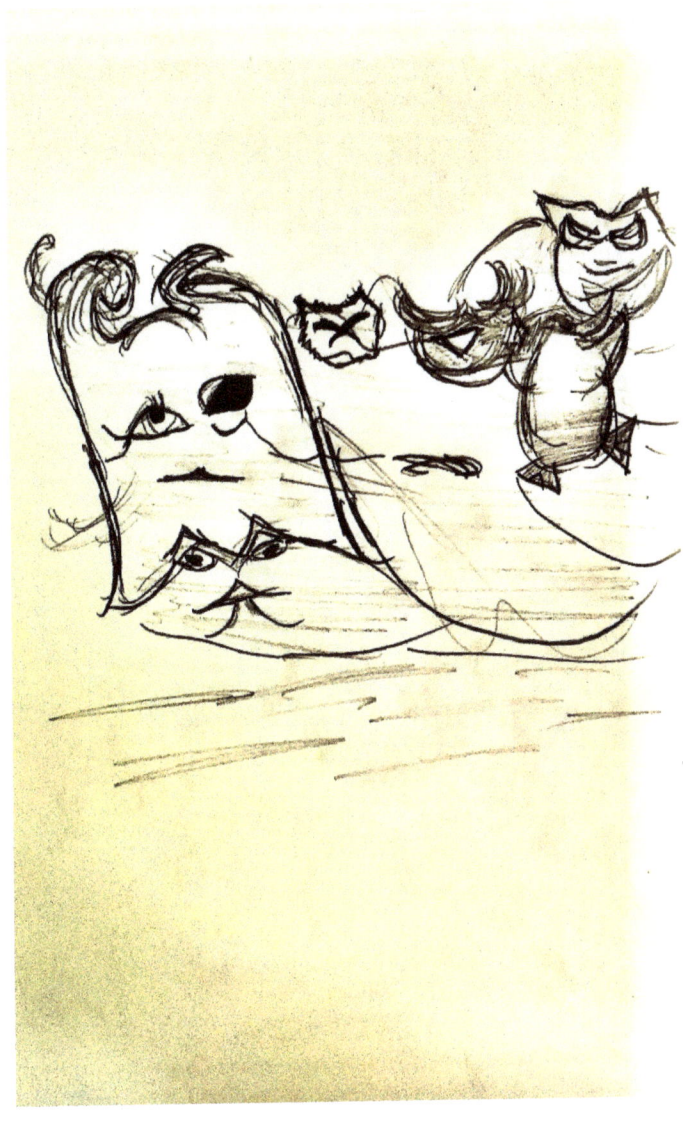

# Cloudy Imaginings

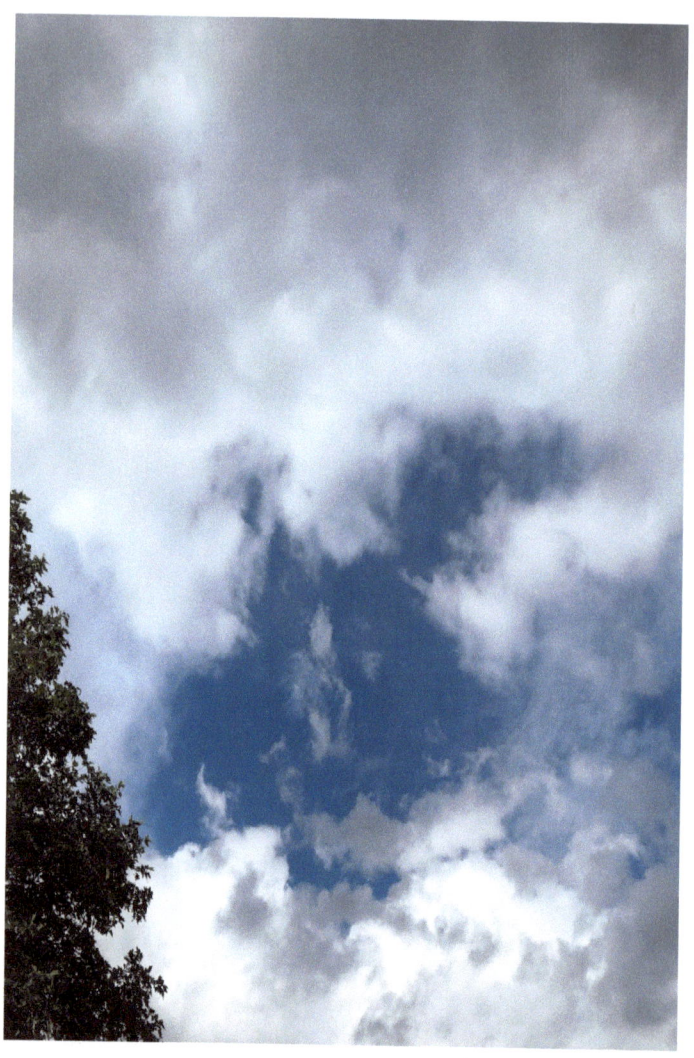

Cloudy Imaginings

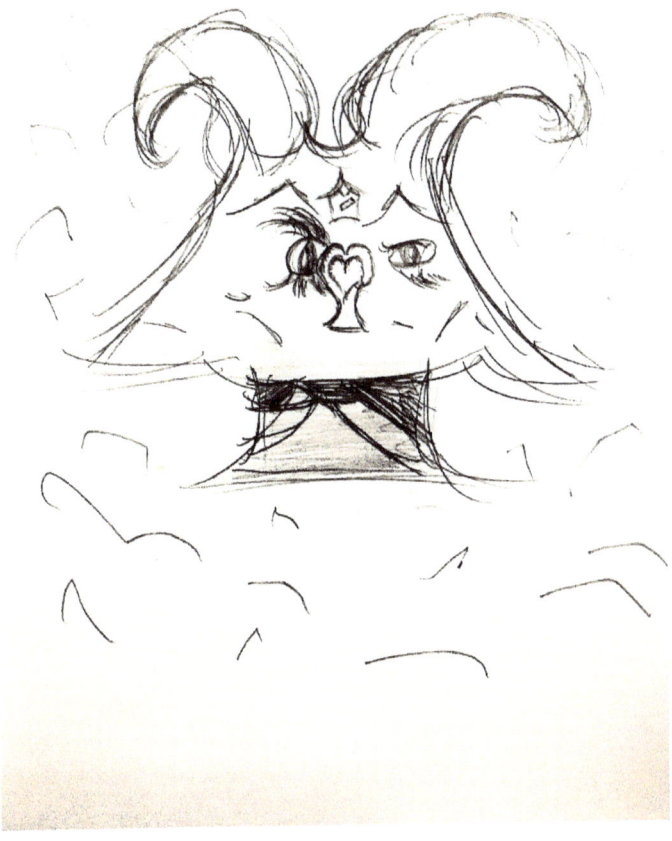

# Cloudy Imaginings

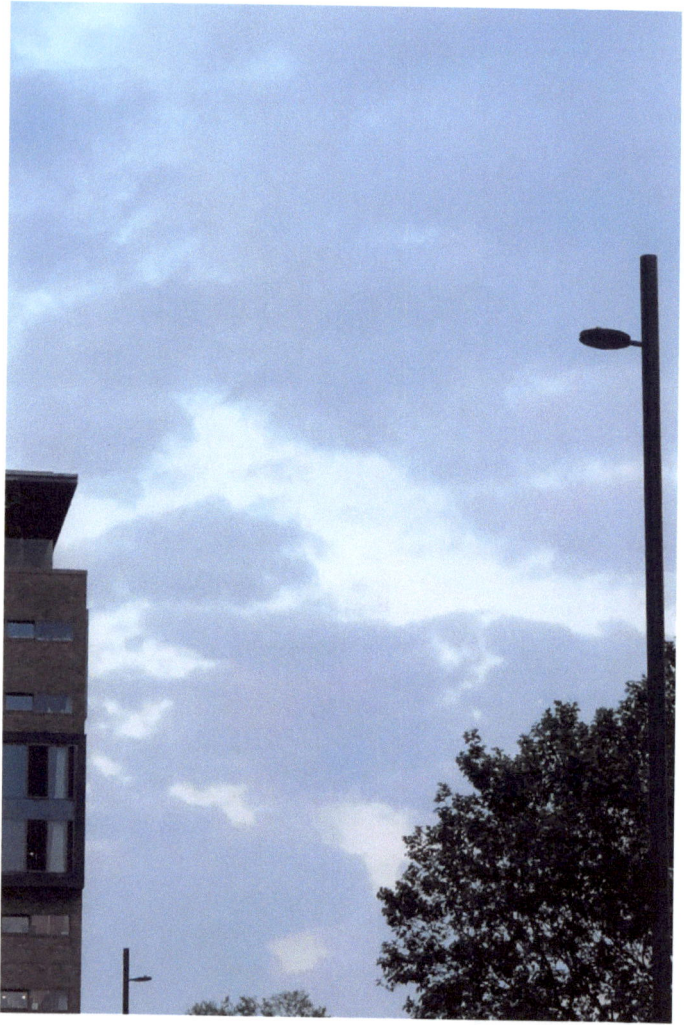

Cloudy Imaginings

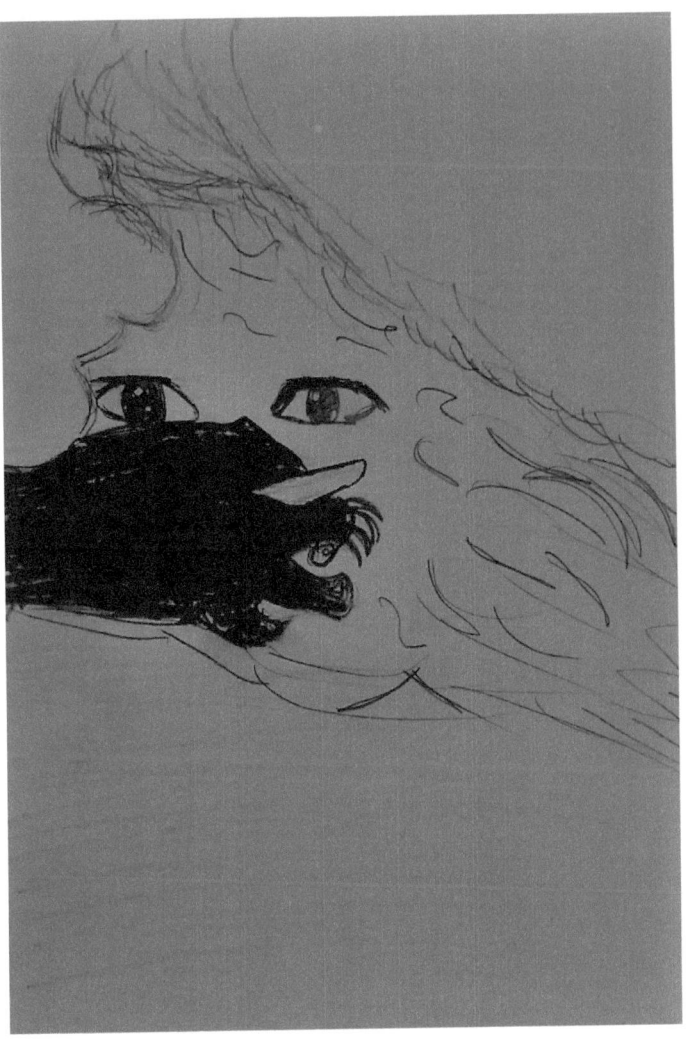

# Cloudy Imaginings

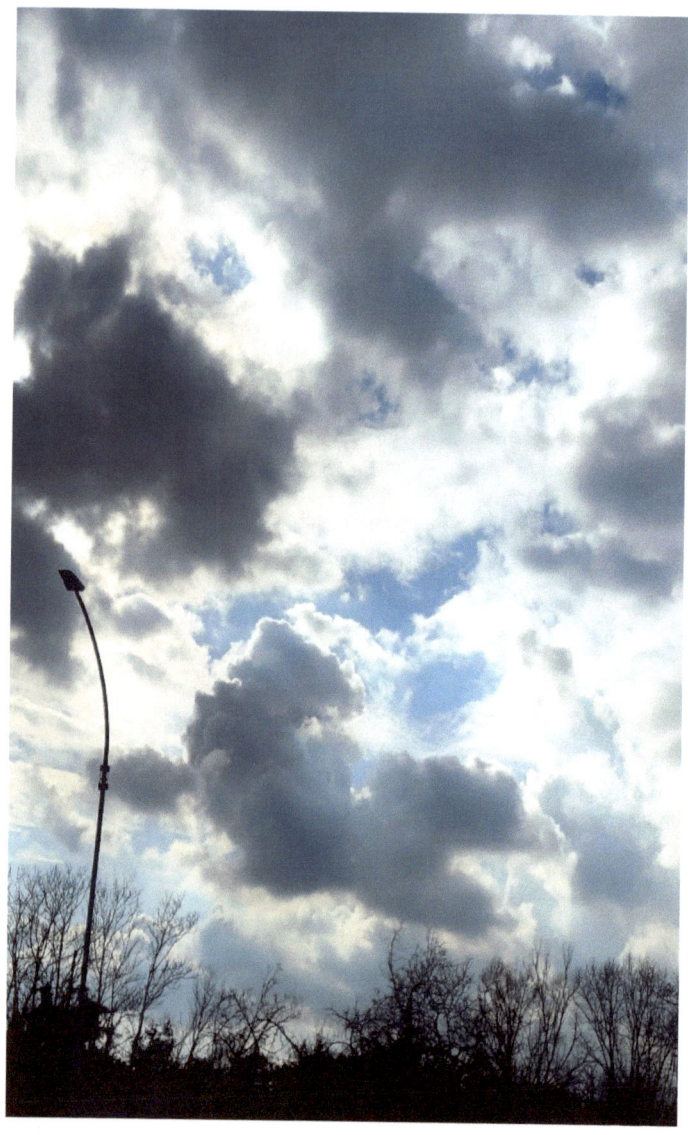

# Cloudy Imaginings

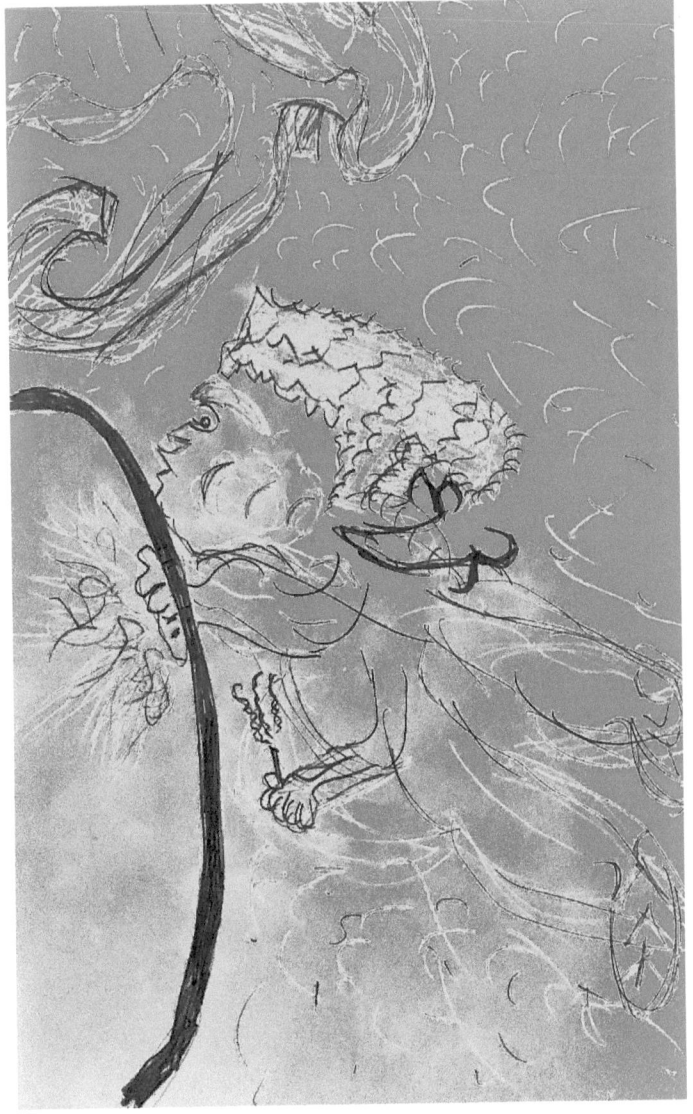

# Cloudy Imaginings

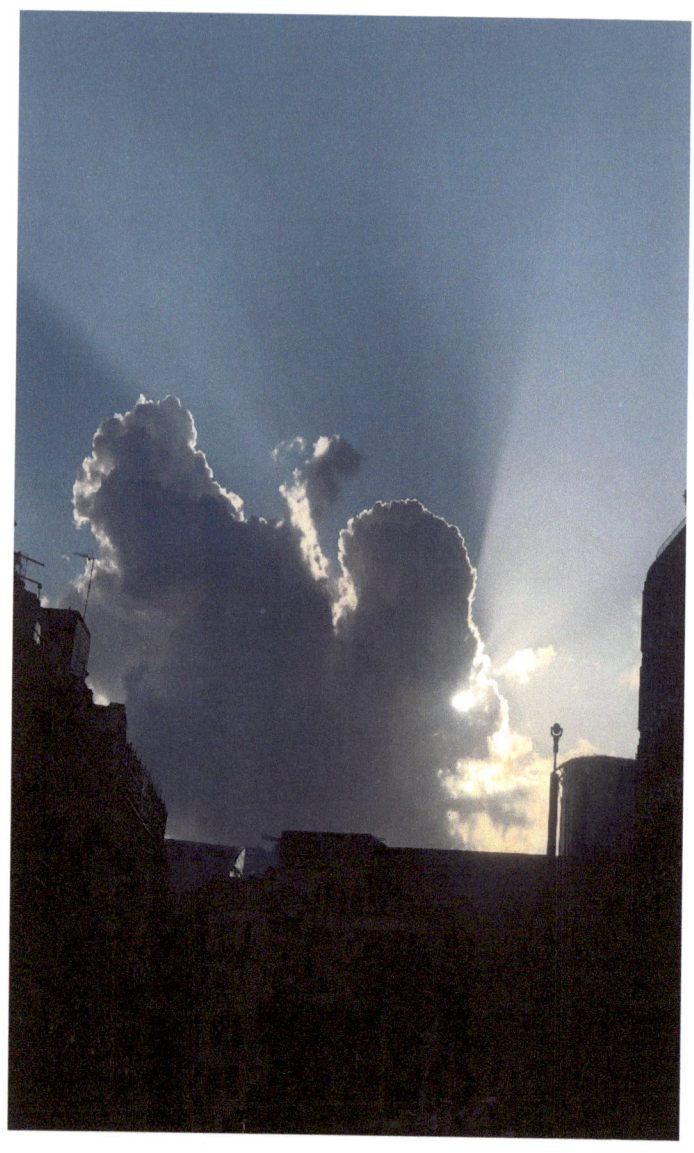

## Cloudy Imaginings

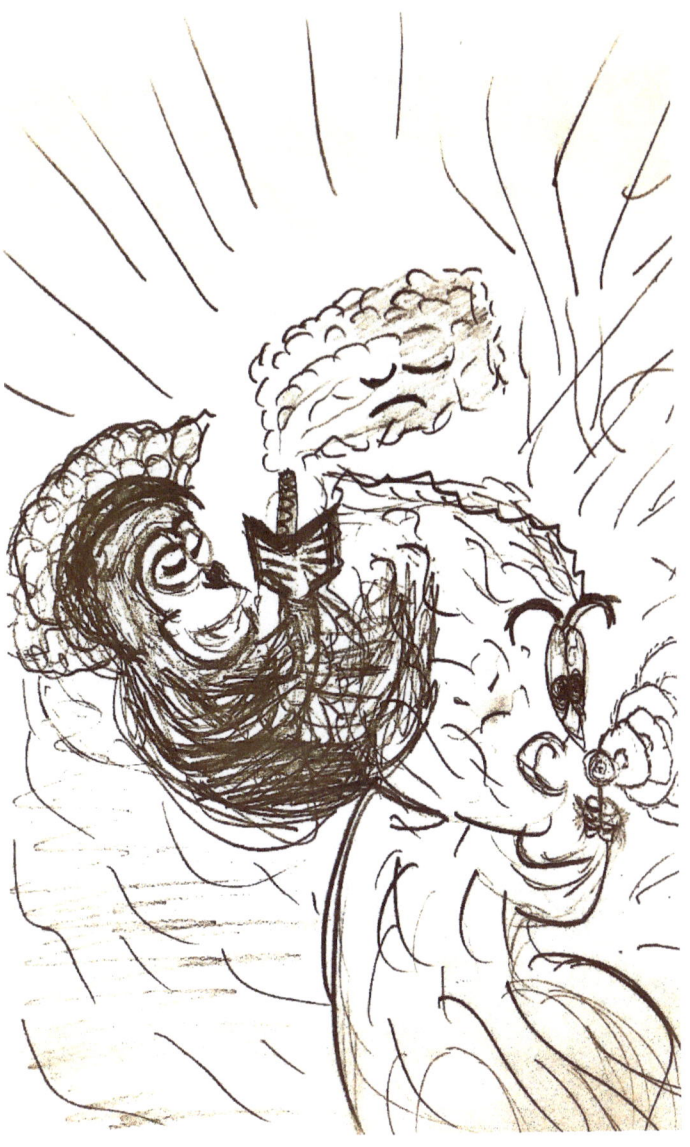

# Cloudy Imaginings

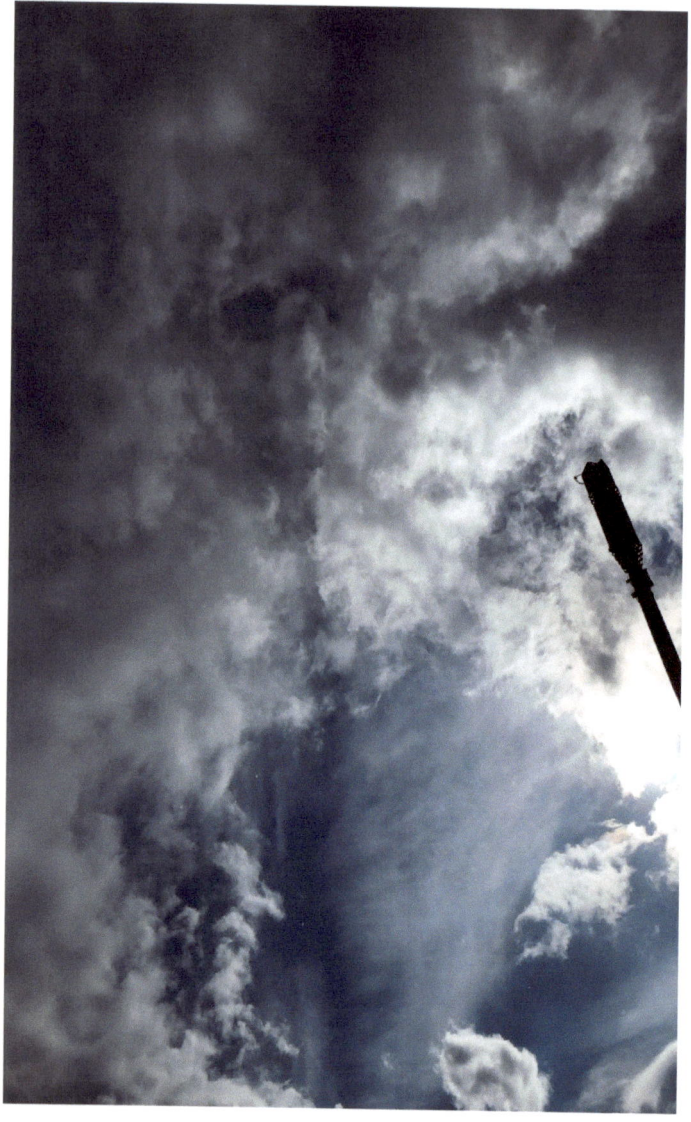

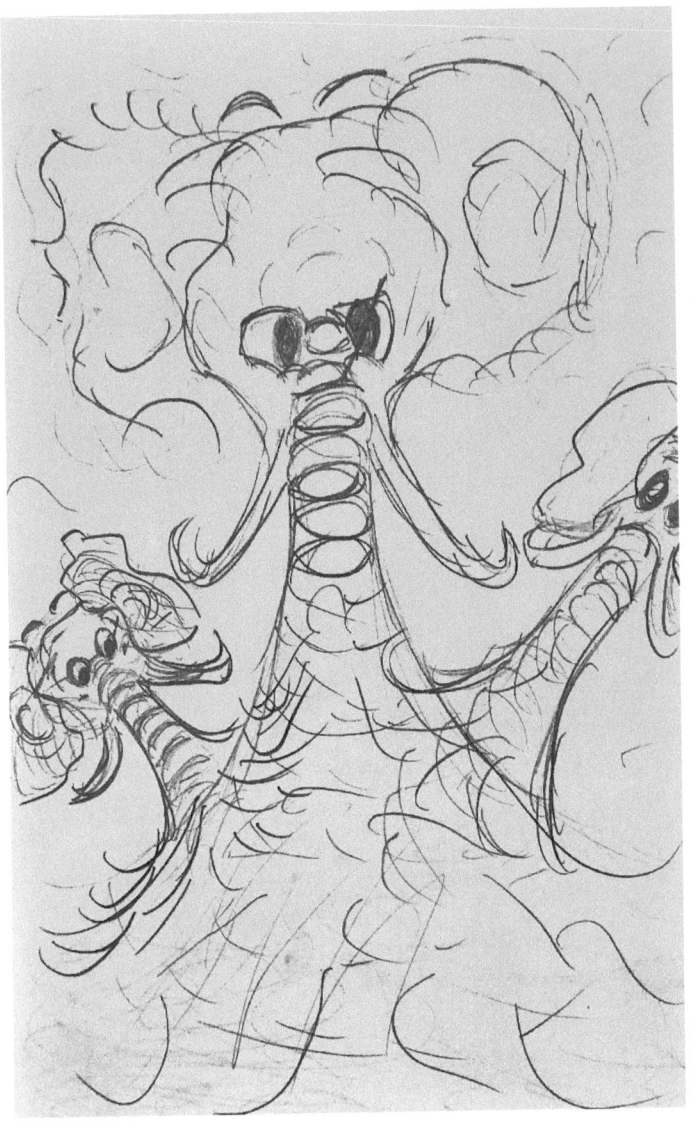

# Cloudy Imaginings

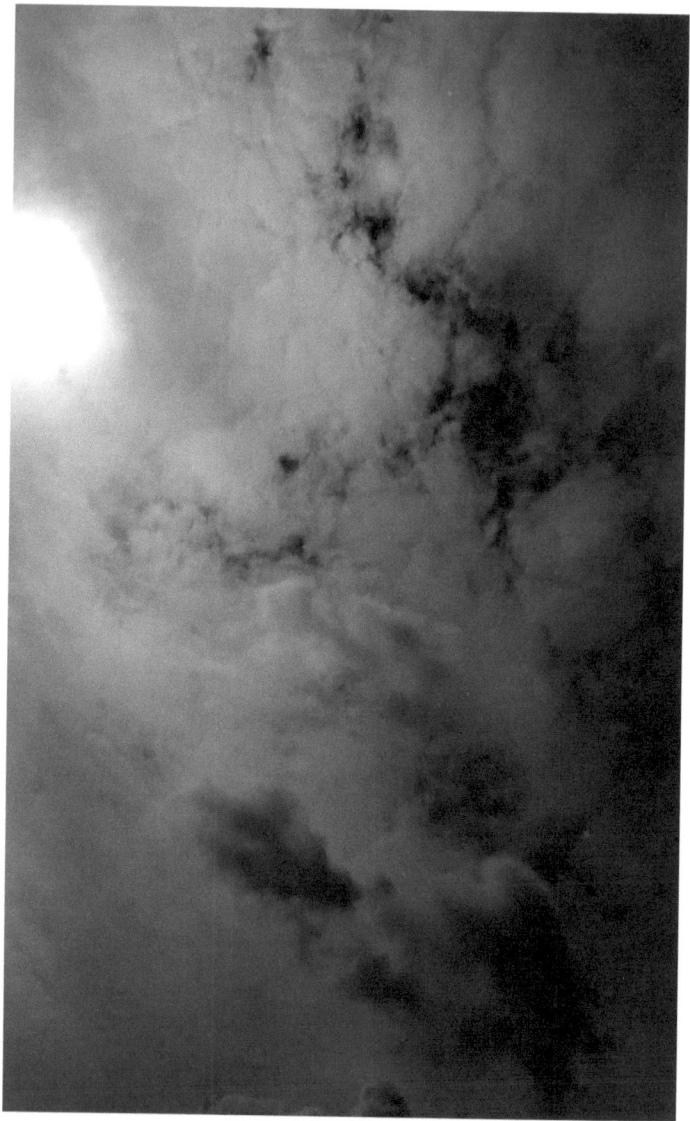

# Cloudy Imaginings

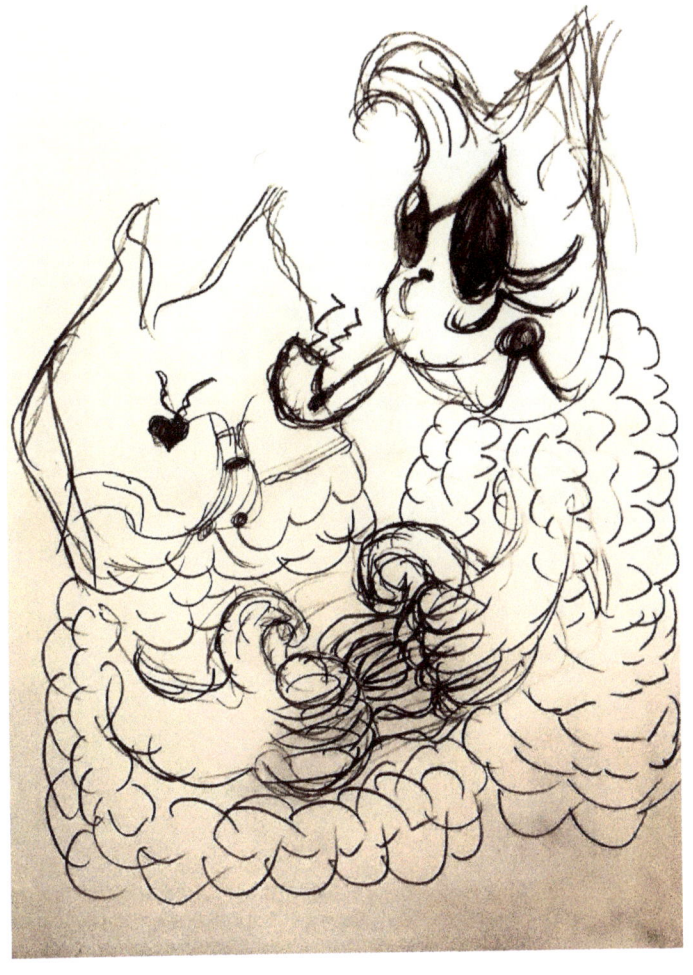

# Cloudy Imaginings

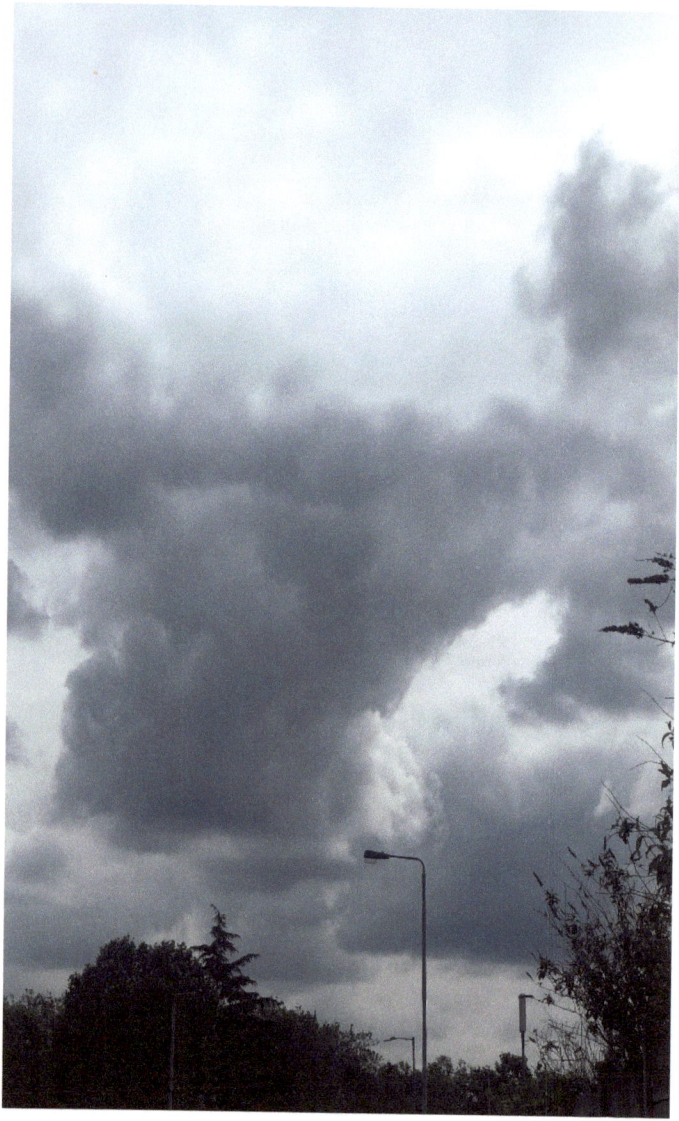

Cloudy Imaginings

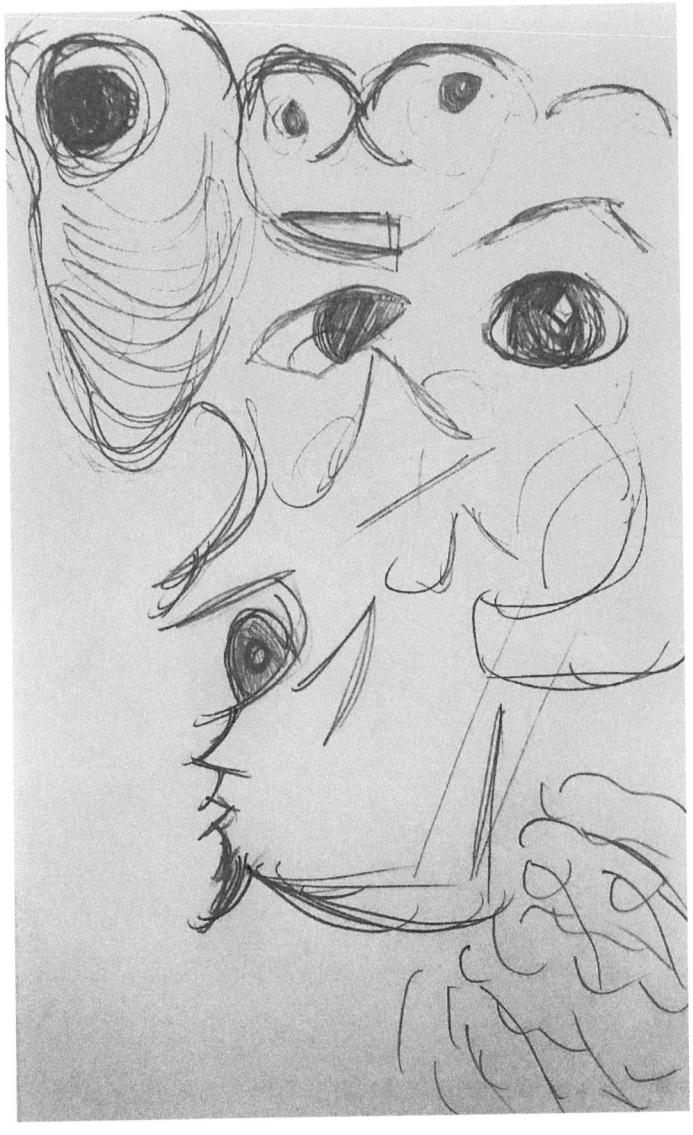

# Cloudy Imaginings

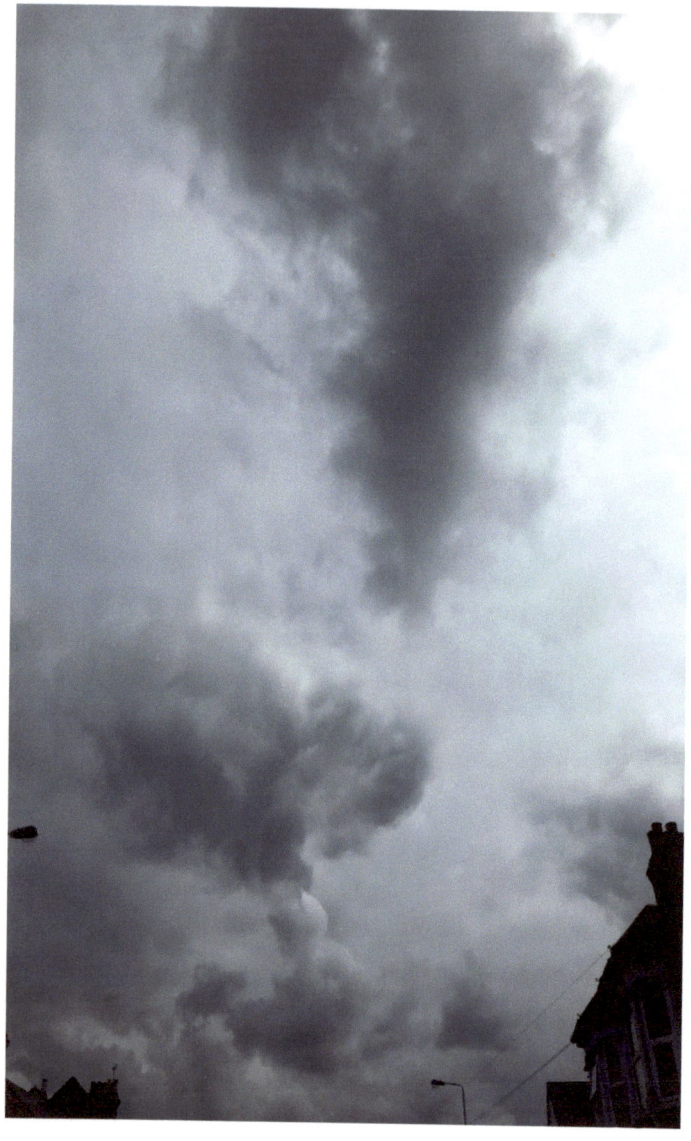

Cloudy Imaginings

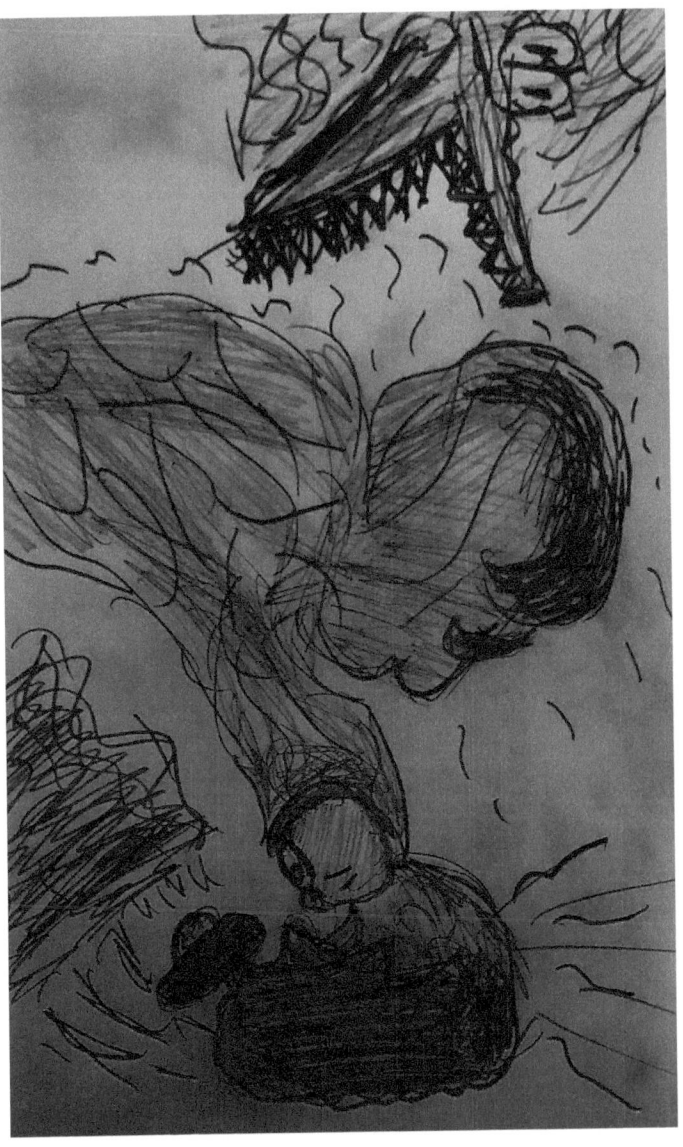

Cloudy Imaginings

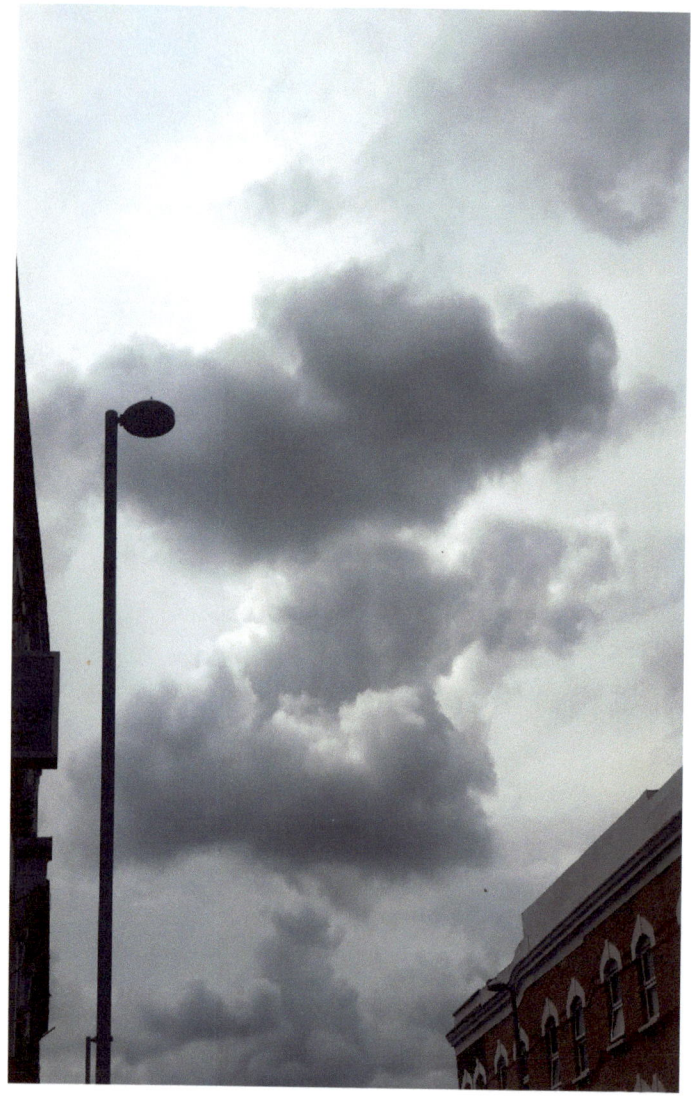

Cloudy Imaginings

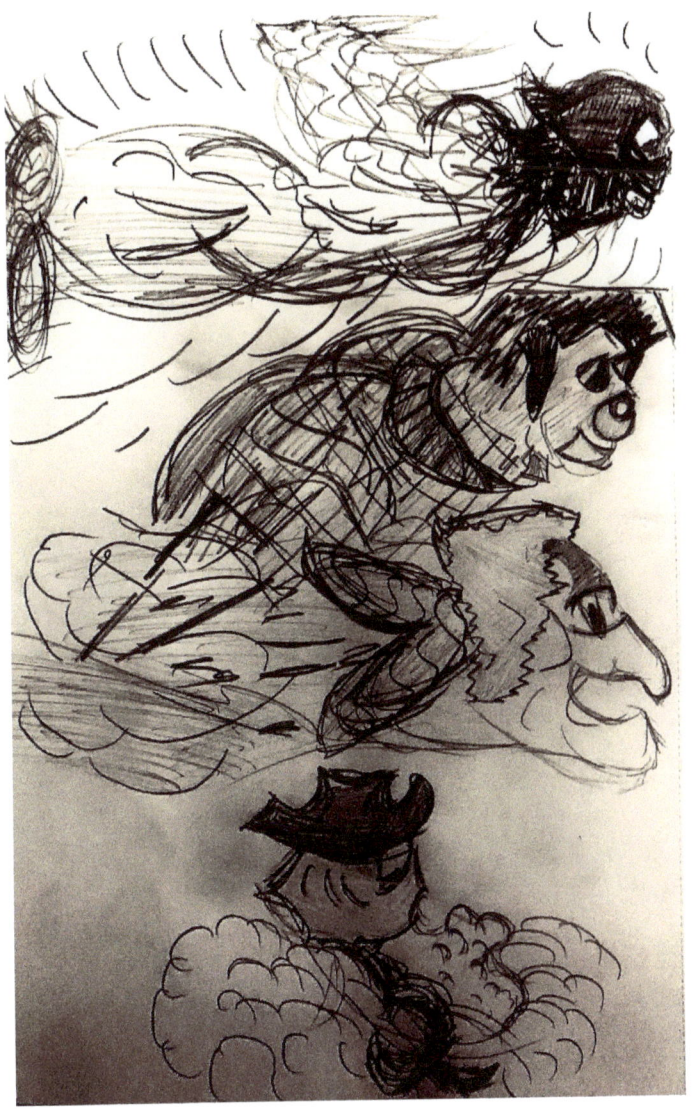

# Cloudy Imaginings

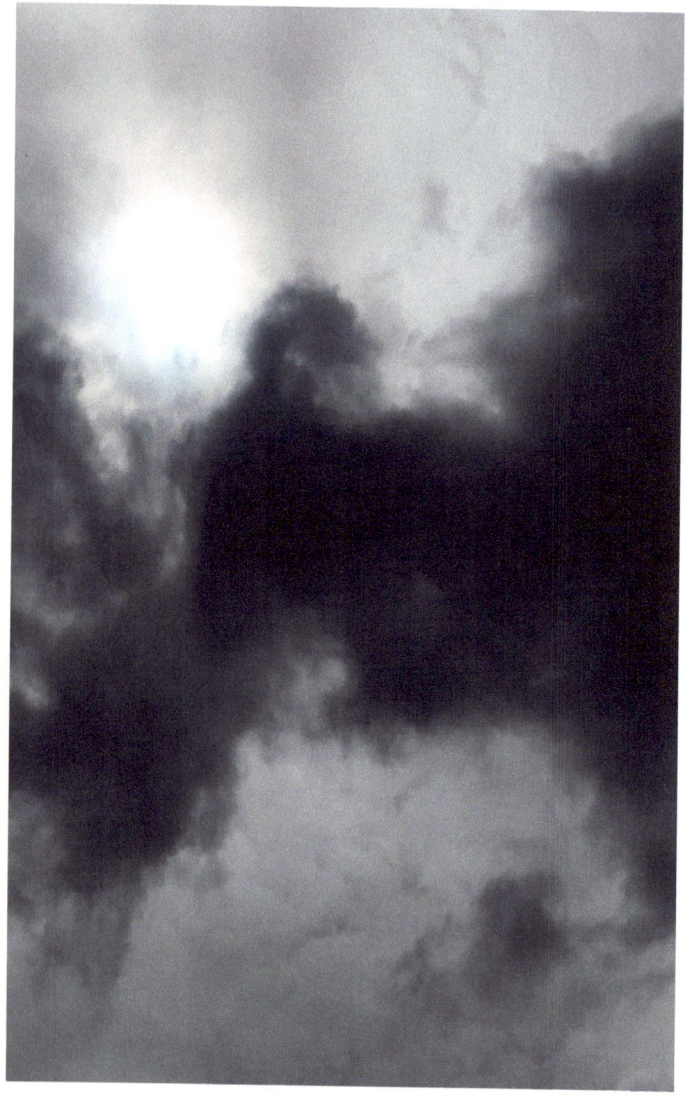

Cloudy Imaginings

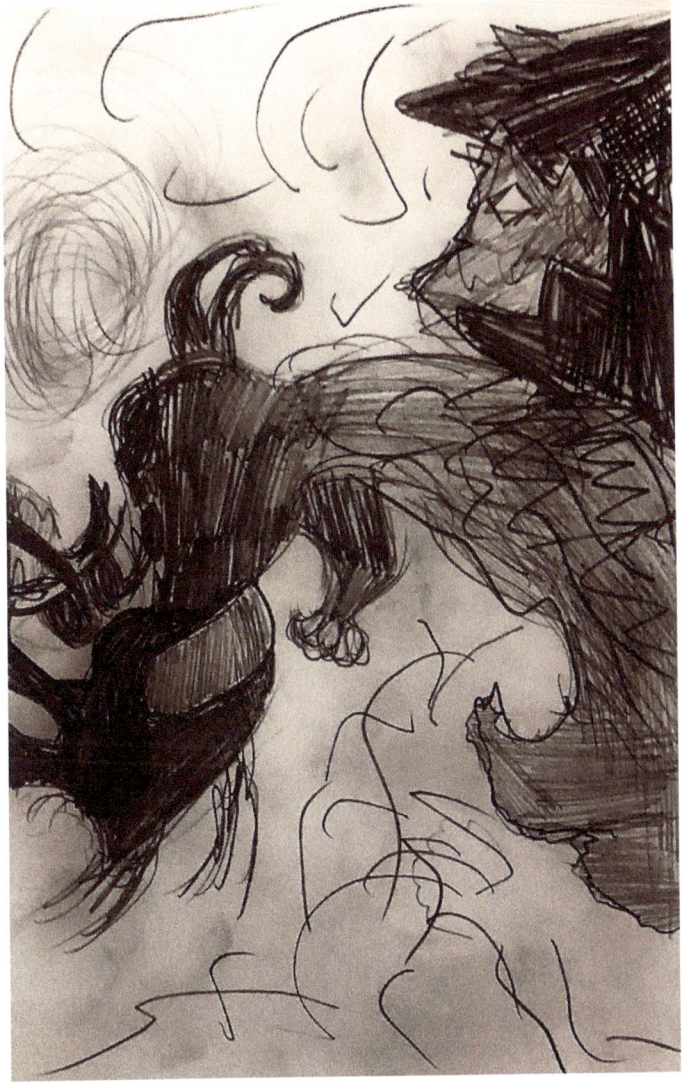

Cloudy Imaginings

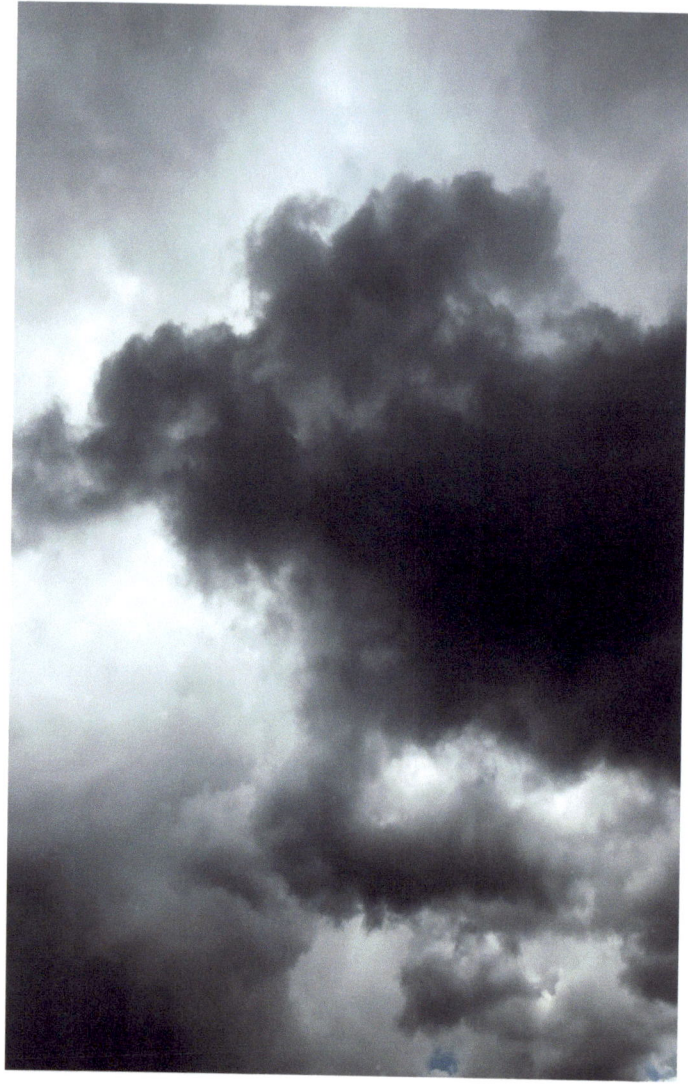

# Cloudy Imaginings

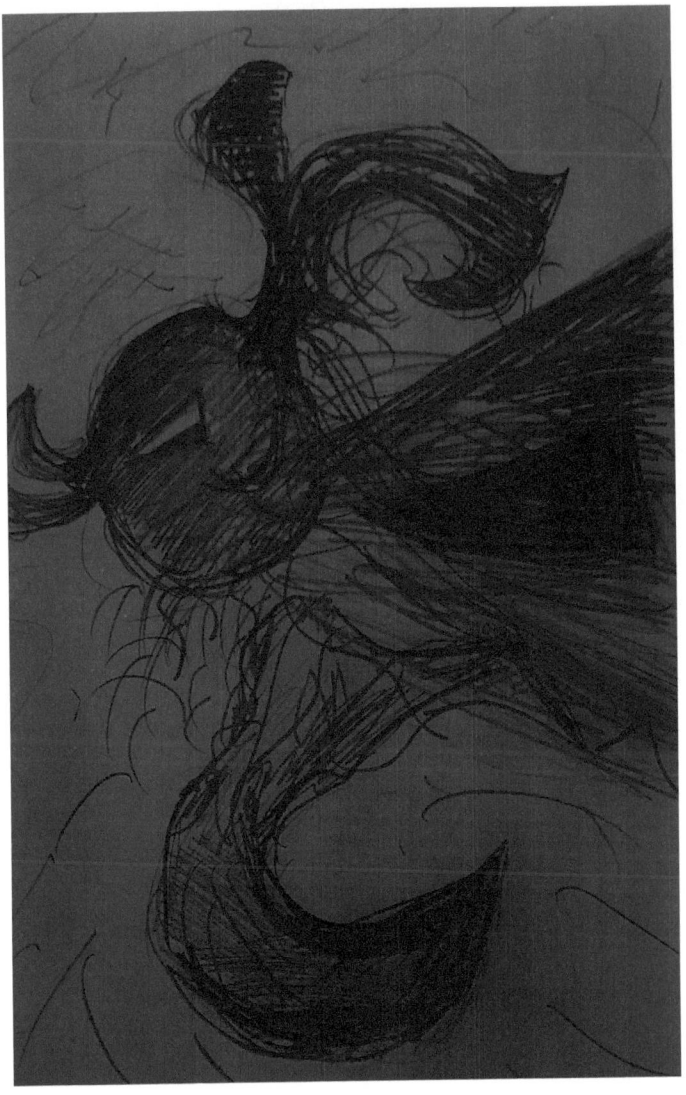

Cloudy Imaginings

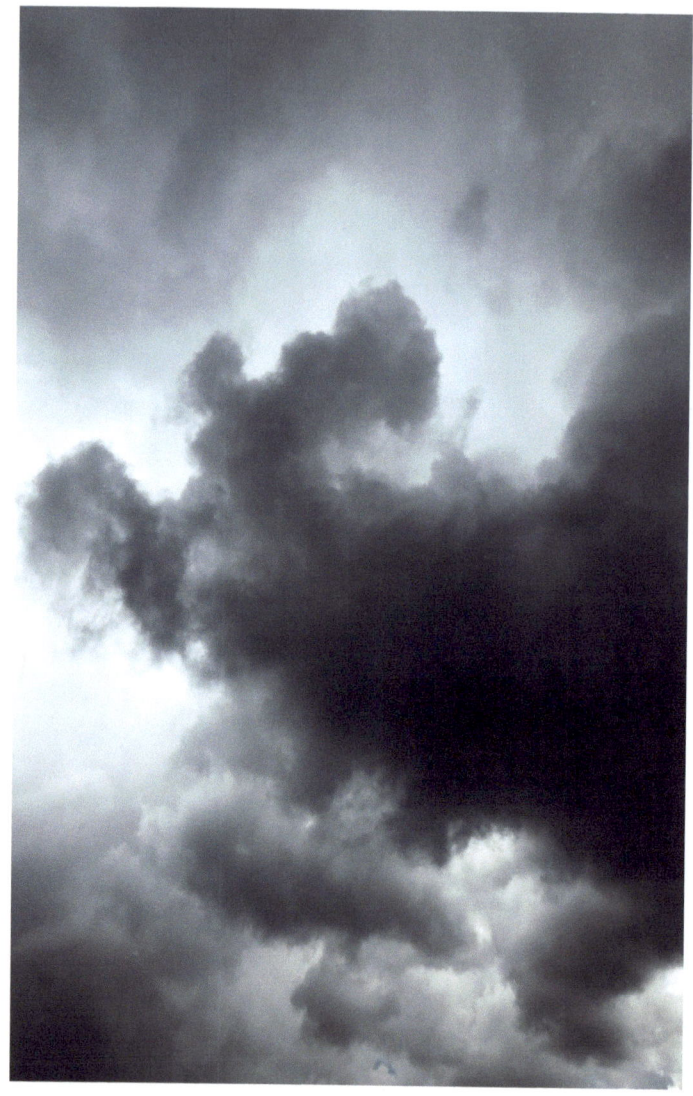

Cloudy Imaginings

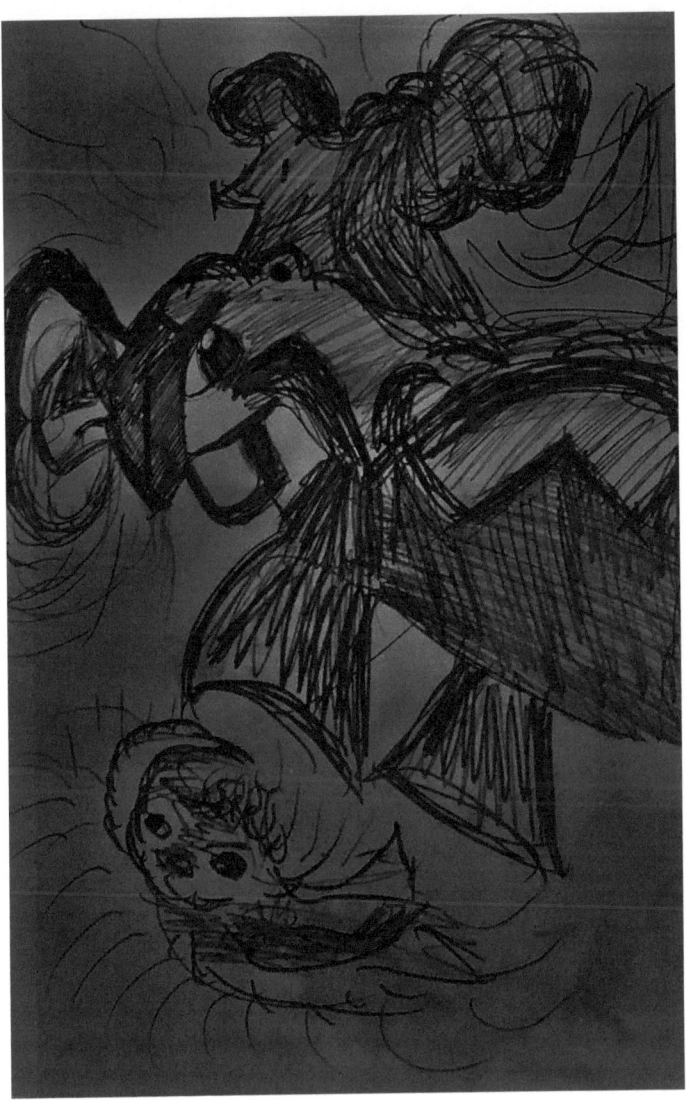

# Cloudy Imaginings

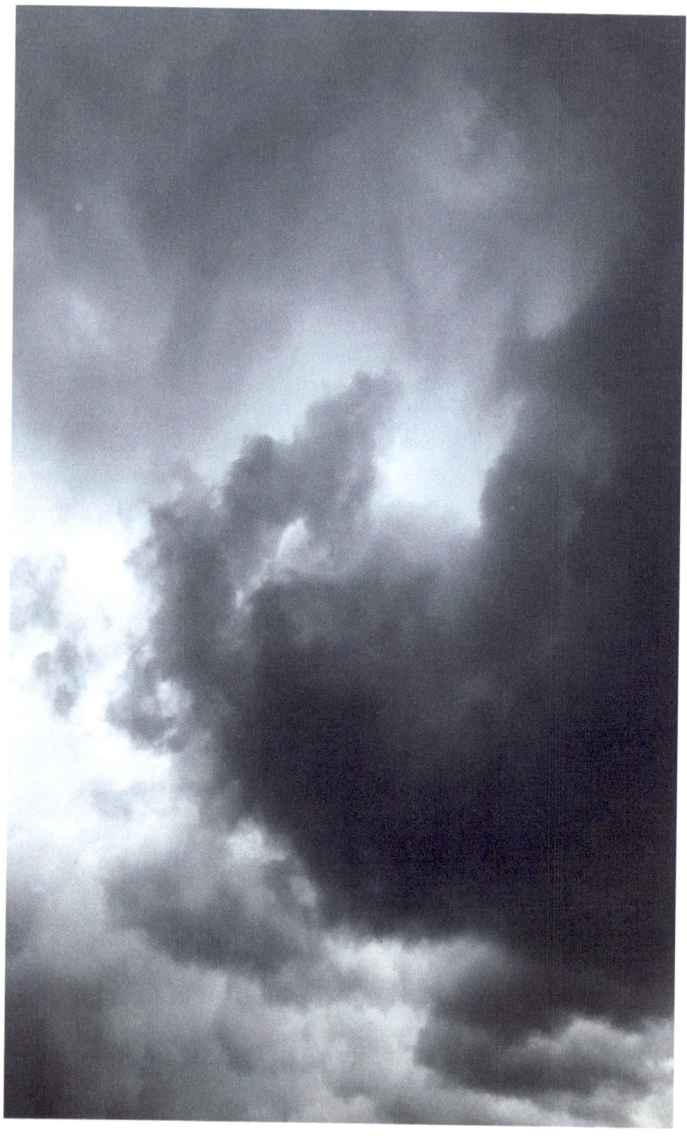

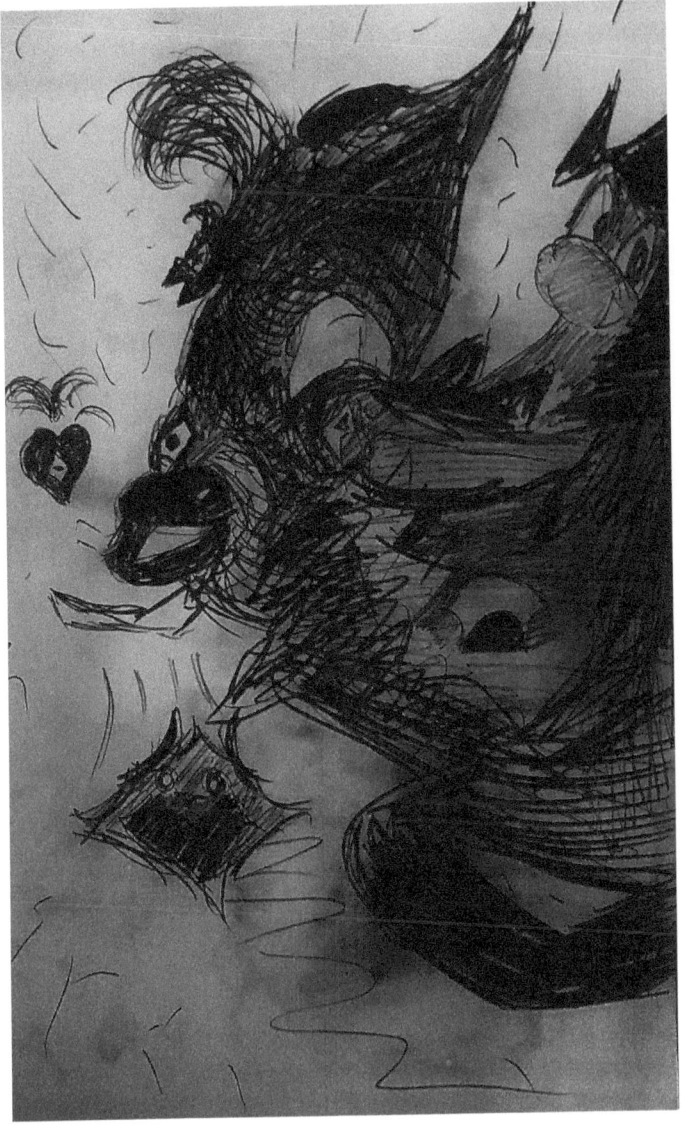

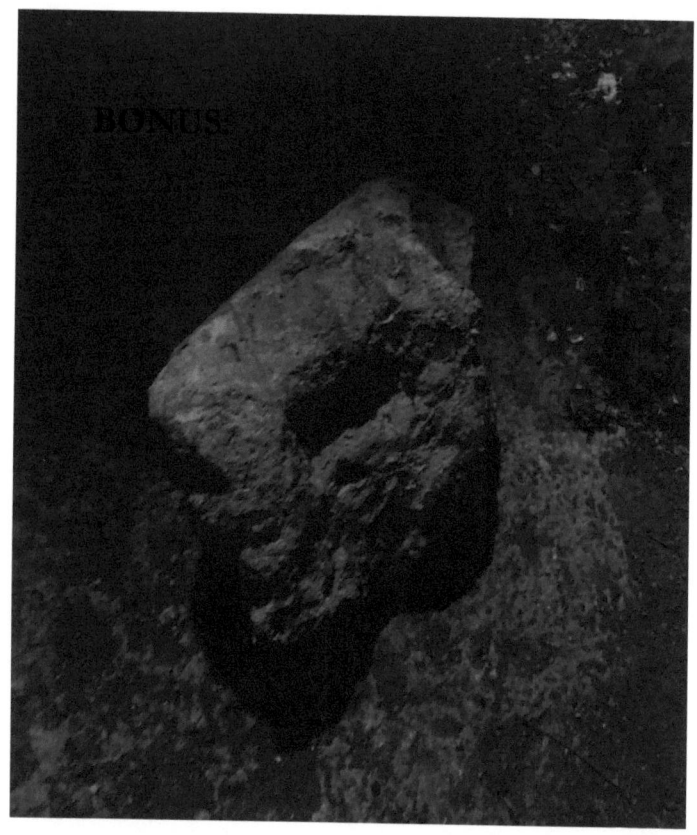

Cloudy Imaginings

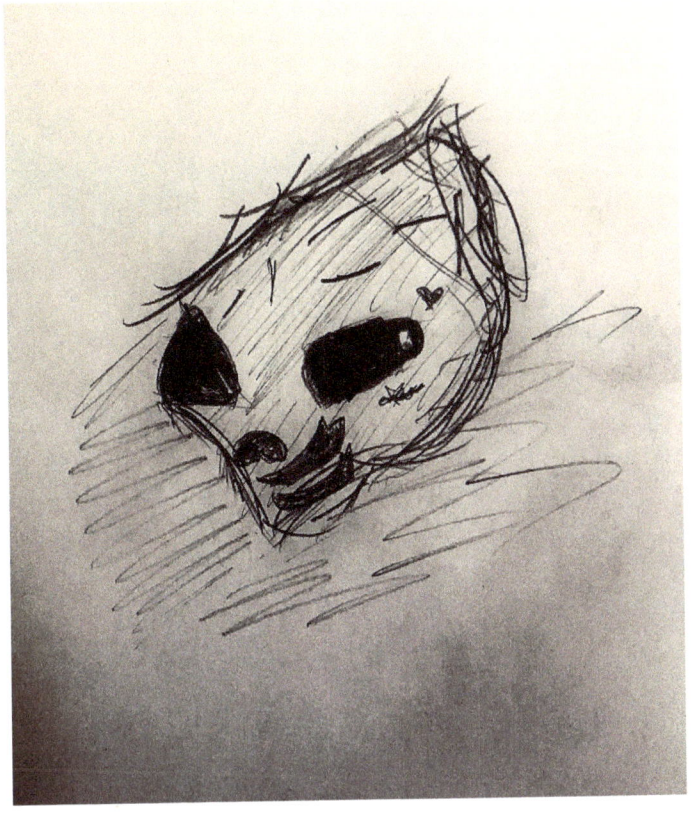

Cloudy Imaginings

TENKU

Cloudy Imaginings

END

www.ingramcontent.com/pod-product-compliance
Lightning Source LLC
Chambersburg PA
CBHW040758240526
45474CB00008B/92